PF
TOO GO

MW01245753

I'm forever grateful for God introducing me to Keith Toogood. The first time I heard Keith talk at BOOM, I felt like the scales fell off my eyes at thirty-four years old. I had always viewed my gifts only as a business owner. That he blessed me with gifts on how to scale a company and make money. I viewed that as my only obligation to the church was to write a check once a month. Or that's maybe how I justified my lack of servant leadership.

I heard a businessman challenging me in business terminology but covered in God's love and scripture to back it up. It has since been a huge step for me in my spiritual growth. As I grew as a leader, we have completely redone our mission, purpose statement and core values.

—Derrick Merchant
CEO of 7B Building & Development

Keith shares his journey in a compelling way that draws the reader into his life and world. In the process, he manages to share his testimony with honesty and humor and demonstrates life lessons learned through experience. This book is a powerful read and opens new possibilities and principles in doing business God's way. One soon realizes that business-people are working people! Normal people! But also people on a mission! The challenges, the price, and the reward of kingdom living are found in every chapter of the book. The adventurous walk with the Holy Spirit is inspiring and challenges you to look at your own journey and once again commit yourself to doing better. If you believe in leaving a lasting legacy, this is the book you must read.

—Kobus Grobler
Missionary and CEO of EMIT, South Africa

Here comes the BOOM! It's not going to be comfortable. But Keith Toogood's story is a real-life reminder of the great cost and even greater reward of following Jesus at the epicenter of the BOOM! I pray God uses this book to inspire many more generations of business leaders who will operate on mission to advance His kingdom.

—Corbin Young
Texas Regional Director, FCA

An inspiring account of personal growth and resilience. The determination to succeed, coupled with faith and good mentors, make for a compelling read.

—Boniface "B.B." Shonga
Bishop-Rock of Hope Assemblies, Zambia, DRC
and Namibia

"Too Good To Be True" is not only a story about one man's journey, but a call to a generation. Businessmen and women have a calling and place in the kingdom when they can see their God-given potential and purpose. Keith lives and breathes the words on these pages! This is his story. But, likely, you'll also

see yourself in this story. May we all live each day operating on mission for our great God and see that life truly is too good to be true!

—**Brad Ingram**
Hillside Christian Church Pastor

The pure emotion and authenticity Keith has shared here is inspiring. Stories of heartbreak, stories of worry and anxiety, stories of triumph that only God can bring. The words on these pages are real life for us all. How do we all take our own stories and bring them into action in our daily life?

Our call to kingdom business is unlocked by the will and mercy of God when we open our hearts to him. Whether you're in discovery mode for what God has for you or you're searching for the next step to bring heaven to earth in your business, this book can be your launching pad. Keith, thank you for your words of wisdom and your boldness to call us all into a deeper relationship with Christ in the workplace.

—**Cole Whisenhunt**
CEO Whisenhunt Group

TOO
GOOD
TO BE
TRUE

TOO
GOOD
TO BE
TRUE

A Call to Kingdom Business

KEITH C. TOOGOOD

ILLUMIFY
MEDIA.COM

Published by
Illumify Media Global
www.IllumifyMedia.com
"Let's bring your book to life!"

Library of Congress Control Number: 2024908374

Paperback ISBN: 978-1-959099-79-6

Cover design by Debbie Lewis

Printed in the United States of America

To my late dad, Richard "Ed" Toogood: The impact you had on my life is truly inconceivable. Your passion for coaching and helping people reach their full potential is a legacy worthy of being carried on.

"A good man leaves an inheritance for their children's children" (Proverbs 13:22).

To my beautiful wife, Brandi: Thank you for going on this crazy, wild goose chase of a journey with me! Eleven places to call home in sixteen years of marriage is, well, insane, but God knew you and I were the perfect pairing as we pursue His kingdom call on our lives. I love you more than you could ever know.

"He who finds a wife finds what is good and receives favor from the LORD" (Proverbs 18:22).

CONTENTS

FOREWORD

Keith Toogood or as we call him "2Good" is a brother, a friend, a motivator, and a trailblazer for this generation. Having had the pleasure of spending many hours fellowshipping with him over the course of the past few years, it is clear that he has been handpicked by God to do his work for his kingdom. In the many facets of his work through BOOM (Business Operating On Mission) and the Epicenter podcast, Keith has revealed himself as a true soldier of the kingdom. He's devoted to leading men and women of all ages to Christ. His latest work is a valuable tool to those of us seeking to do the same.

Too Good to Be True helped me better understand not only 2Good the man but also the Christ in him. It takes the reader on a journey of a life lived fully and faithfully—the ups, the downs, the smiles, the cries. Toogood artfully shares his testimony and the lessons he learned over the years in a way that presents a constant reminder that Christ dwells in every detail, and a humbling realization that God is ultimately in control (even when we think we are)!

Spoiler Alert: My favorite part of the journey is when he shares how after completing college and becoming a successful businessman with a picture-perfect plan laid out for his life, he hears the voice of God say, "sell everything and follow Me." Life can be a roller-coaster of uncertainty—you doubt, you worry, you live in your mind five years ahead of time instead of the moment at hand. But the life of a man who has chosen to walk in faith is often even more challenging. With God giving you only a few directions at a time, anxiety tries every nook and cranny attempting to shake your foundation.

Toogood takes readers alongside him as he learns to walk by faith and not by sight.

Many of us are now confronted with the question of "how do we raise a generation of young men and women on the principles of Christ when there's so many distractions in today's world threatening to lead them in the opposite direction of Him?" This book is a great guide. Packed with biblical nugget after biblical nugget, it constantly reminds the reader that no man is perfect aside from Jesus Christ. As human beings we *will* make mistakes, but the grace and forgiveness through the cross is for all of us. Most important, it delivers a powerful gut punch to fear where it stands as a true testimony of the fact that God has a plan for all of our lives. I read this entire book in less than twenty-four hours, and I plan to read it again. I'm encouraged to know that I have another brother in faith walking this life with me. I pray that this book blesses you the same way.

At the end of the day, the ultimate purpose of life is to teach the gospel of Jesus Christ and draw souls to the kingdom of God. *Too Good to Be True* shares Keith's inspiring journey so masterfully that even those who may have never picked up a Bible a day in their lives will find themselves ready to take up their crosses. This book is for parents, for husbands and wives, for teachers and coaches, for men and women in business, for the young person unsure of the future, and for the rest of us who enjoy being reminded that God is not done. The power of the blood has not faded, and God is actively working it all out for you.

To our brother, Toogood, and your family—we are honored to know you and consider you as family.

J. Long and Cyntoia Brown-Long

INTRODUCTION

My hilarious, beautiful wife, Brandi, was uber concerned about the title of the book when I shared it with her for the first time. She was genuinely concerned you wouldn't pick it up like it was some kind of bad dad joke—a corny play on words. She said, "This is a book about binness!" Yes, that's how she affectionately refers to what everyone else in the world calls business. But I had to; it was too good to pass up. See what I did there?

Alright, alright, all bad dad jokes aside, the journey you're about to embark on with this book, and the revelation I pray God brings your way, truly is too good to be true. It transcends logic. It gives you freedom to live as a new creation in a world that's constantly looking for sameness. My prayer is that through this book, you're set free to realize the God-given potential that lies deep inside those bones of yours. If you're a businessperson, this book is for you. If you are a pastor, I pray that this book helps you to see more clearly the deep wiring God has for those outside of vocational ministry. And if you're a stay-at-home mom, or someone who works in the service industry who doesn't see themselves as a businessperson, I pray that part one of this book, along with chapter 18, sets your spirit on fire as you read my story—my testimony. Many have told me it's too good to be true, as it awakens the God-given potential in their life.

Just to set the record straight, Toogood really is my last name. And yes, I've heard it all. It was always quite comical to see the opposing fans try and come up with something I had never heard when I played football at Texas Tech. They'd try and mess with me or get in my head, but I'd just ignore them because not one of them ever came up with anything new or innovative. At one point, I turned around and said, "I've heard them all. Once you come up with something you think I've never heard, then let me know." They never said another word for the rest of the game because they just weren't that creative.

A last name like mine is a prime target, and, without a doubt, the primer to a lot of great conversations. In jest, people have called me Keith No Good, Dos Bueno, Too Bad, Toogood Three Bad, and of course Toogood to be true. I thought I had heard every possible variation until one of my former teammates topped them all when he looked me dead in the eye and said, "You're not too good. You're just okay." Of course, he was kidding, I think. As you can imagine, my name has garnered some attention, and quite a bit of fun has been had with it over the years. People often look at me when they hear it for the first time and ask, "Is that really your last name? That's pretty fun!" Inevitably I shoot back, "It's fun until something doesn't go right. Then it's not really all that fun." That usually garners a little chuckle, and we move on to the task at hand and the reason for our meeting.

My middle name seems to garner a reaction, as well. I used to be embarrassed of my middle name when I was a boy, mostly because of the attention I got from it, but it's now something that I'm incredibly proud of. That *C* that you may have seen on the front of the book stands for Crockett. That bloodline runs through my mom's side of the family, and I'll go ahead and answer the question now: yes, I am kin to Davy Crockett—yes, *the* Davy Crockett—one of the heroes from the battle of the Alamo and a key cog to sending Texas on the path of gaining its independence. Davy was a man who was unafraid and unashamed to stand for what he believed to be right. Many would venture to say a man's man, a man on a mission.

Then there is my first name, Keith. I am the namesake of one of my dad's favorite soccer players when he was a coach at North Mesquite High School back in the 1970s. I don't know much about the Keith from my dad's time, but I know my dad respected him as an upstanding young man. The name Keith has a Celtic origin and means "warrior descending," while the Old Welsh meaning is "from the forest/wilderness." Its inherent meaning is "from the place of battle," and its spiritual meaning is "brave."

That's my identity here on this earth. It's on my birth certificate, driver's license, and Social Security card. That's how people know me. But what if I told you that God has reidentified me as he added to my earthly identity with his heavenly identity? We see him change people's names all throughout Scripture, but it's like we have relegated that to some ancient practice that doesn't happen today. But what if I told you that God wants you to know your kingdom identity? What if I told you that God has a greater purpose for your life? That's exactly what he did with me, but in order to get there he had to take me through a process. He had to test me. He had to shape me and mold me into who he desired me to be. And let me tell you, he didn't do that for my sake or my glory—no, he did it for his sake. He doesn't shape us and mold us for our glory but for his. He will not let himself be defamed. He will not yield his glory to another!

So here is what you need to know about me.

I'm just a normal dude—really no different than you. I'm sure my day looks and feels much like yours: there's the battle to provide for my family; to lead our organizations through the treacherous waters of the ocean we like to call business; to keep my body physically fit and my mind sharp; and to lead my family into a deepening relationship with our Lord and Savior, Jesus Christ. What's more, it took over four years to write this book. For close to three of those years, though, I ran the other way. I was scared. Yet through it all, every time I'd wander, I found God continually bringing me back to the pages of this book. He knew I would run; he knows me well. Yet I rest in the truth that this book arrived to you with impeccable timing because God is never late. He is always on time.

Here is some more you need to know: I've never been to seminary, I don't pastor a church, and I don't hold degrees in philosophy or psychology. Please don't cancel me yet because as you'll see later in this book, none of those are a qualifier to do God's kingdom work. Is a deep understanding of God, Jesus, Holy Spirit, and reverence for God's Holy Word, the Bible, critical to helping others find their way to God's kingdom? Yes! So my prayer is that as you dive into this book, the cloaking of the enemy that says you must have those titles or criteria gets ripped away and you simultaneously find yourself running free in God's kingdom, equipped with Holy Spirit leading the way.

As I wrestled with the title of this book, I went back and forth on what it should be called. Then one of my best friends, J. Long, sent me what I consider to be a prophetic word on September 29, 2023, at 3:55 in the morning. In the text I received from him, one sentence in particular stood out: "This is the book of Toogood to be true." Those words gave me the kick in the pants I needed to finish the book and were undoubtedly an answer to a specific prayer I had put in God's hands. So let me ask you some questions:

Who are you?

Why are you here?

Is there more to your life than you ever knew?

What is your kingdom identity?

These are the questions I pray get answered as you go on this journey with me. My friend and partner in BOOM and incredibly gifted man with a kingdom anointing, Roswell Smith Jr., helped me come up with some meditations and questions to help you work through answers on your journey.

I'm on a mission decreed by God to wake up a generation—specifically, a generation of businesspeople and young men and boys. As you read this book, my prayer is that you step into the BOOM—that you become the epicenter of the BOOM. You may be thinking, *What's the BOOM?* I'm glad you asked. Jump into chapter 1 so that you can find out just who you are in God's kingdom business.

PART 1

MY STORY

1

THE COMFORT

It's not going to be comfortable.

I'm going to step out onto the proverbial limb and venture to say that's probably not the best six words to open a book with if my end game is for people to read a single page beyond this one. But I must. I must start this way because so often that's how Jesus led in. On the other hand, I must lead in this way because of the reward. Oh, how great the reward is. Notice I didn't say how great the reward is going to be. I said how great it is. Present tense. Imperative to note.

I'm uncomfortable. I'm tired. And I'm willing to bet that you are tired too.

Mentally. Physically. Emotionally. Spiritually. As businesspeople, the struggles we've faced post-covid pushed us to our limits.

As the leader of four business ventures and a ministry, I've done everything I can to please my employees, my clients, my vendors, and so many more. And when I say everything, I truly mean everything. And if my view of the world is mostly accurate, I'd venture to say that is the goal of every organizational leader regardless of the company size. If it wasn't, businesses would be folding up faster than a cheap lawn chair on a breezy summer day.

Over the last three years, I've been through it. Man, I've been through it. Yet at the exact same time, I find myself filled like never before. The juxtaposition. I've been slandered on social media by the people of a town where I don't even lay my head each night, yet at the same time, I've received text messages from men well into the evening telling me how the conversation we had earlier that day had renewed their spirit and spurred them on; transformation of the heart, soul, and mind was underway as the master heart surgeon, God, did his work. I've had clients chew me up and spit me out, and at the exact same time, I've had clients lavish us with praise stacked upon praise about how wonderful of an experience they had with one of our companies. I've had employees who have raved about the work environment and how they absolutely love working for one of our teams only to be shredded to pieces on social media by former employees who felt an injustice when it came to their discharge from one of our companies.

It's been polarizing to say the least.

I've got people who love me, and I've got people who may very well hate me. And for a guy who's done everything he can to uphold Romans 12:18 which says, "If it is possible, as far as it depends on you, live at peace with everyone," that can be a difficult pill to swallow. But through it all, as I'm tossed around in these treacherous waters we like to call business, I've learned, and continue to learn, to center myself in Christ.

Before I go any further, please know that this isn't some plea for you to feel sorry for me like I'm some sort of victim of my circumstances. That's not the case at all. Don't get me wrong, there have been times where I've wanted to curl up in a corner and hide. I am just human after all. I've wanted to quit. I've wanted to slam shut the doors that the Lord himself had ushered me through. I've tried to act on it—this book being case number one. I'm like Jonah but much worse. As far as we know, he ran the other way just once. I've run the other way many times over. It's hard to be vulnerable, especially in a world that cancels people for one wrong move, or one perceived wrong move, but then the Lord speaks: "This is what I've called you to. Keep going. I've got you."

I'll say it again: it's not going to be comfortable.

I recognize that the calling to be an ambassador of Christ is high, that to whom much is given much is required (Luke 12:48), and that the world is going to hate me. Why? Because it hated him first. If I belonged to the world, it would love me as its own. But as I type the very words that appear on this page, I recognize that I do not belong to the world because Christ has chosen me out of this world. That is why the world hates me (John 15:18–19). Now for the antidote: He has told me this so that in him I may have peace. Not in my achievements. Not in my bank account. Not in what people think of me. Not in my good works. In him! That's where I'll find my peace! That's where you'll find your peace. And here's a guarantee: in this world we will have trouble. But take heart, Jesus has overcome the world (John 16:33)!

Now let me be real with you. I'm not at all innocent and pure as a snow falling on a chilly winter morning. Far from it. I'll be the first to admit that I'm a sinner. A screwup. An imperfect man who has allowed the weakness of my flesh, and the pride of my heart, to get the best of me. I haven't had to battle alcohol, sexual temptations, pornography, or drugs like we hear so often when it comes to men. That's not how the enemy attacks me. I have had to battle and overcome pride, anger, and bitterness to the very ones who are closest to me. Currently, as all four of my businesses go through unprecedented times, I'm having to learn how to overcome doubt, worry, and fear—a state of mind contrary to what God has called us to as his followers. So what can we gather from this one short list of struggles we face? Regardless of the temptations or attacks, all have fallen short of the glory of God (Romans 3:23). Not just once or twice.

But over.

And over.

And over.

Do you relate to any of this? I'm willing to put my bottom dollar on the line and say that you've experienced many of the same treacherous waters as me, and you and I are more alike than we are different. It took me a long time to truly see my brokenness. As you'll read later, I saw myself as "good," but the older I get, the more I realize what a broken, wretched, messed up man I am. I'm a screwup who doesn't deserve the opportunity to put these words on paper, but I thank God for the shed blood of Christ and his unending grace that has allowed this book to sit in your hands. I thank God for the opportunity to share with you what the King of kings has to say about you and this journey that you find yourself on. I thank God that he isn't finished with me yet. And you need to know, no matter where you find yourself today, he isn't finished with you either.

Back to the reward. You may be thinking to yourself, "Geez, I thought this book was going to be uplifting." Oh, it is. It just may not come in the way you expected. If you are looking for some "get rich quick" strategy that's going to make you money hand over fist, you've got the wrong book. That's called the prosperity gospel, and it's one of the biggest lies of this generation. It's garbage.

Absolute garbage!

Out of the four ventures God had me start in the last nine years, only two of them provided a living for my family and me. The other two have never paid me a dime to date. In fact, one of them was so decimated by COVID that it never recovered. I now have to fund it to keep the doors open, but this is what God has called me to at the present moment. I don't know what the future holds for any of the aforementioned businesses, but I know the Lord holds the keys and that is where I find my peace.

Does God want good for us? Absolutely! He wants us to experience true joy as we walk the road he's invited us on. He wants us to experience a life that we never could have imagined. He wants us to experience freedom in him. But you have to know, and be okay with the fact, that that may not come with worldly wealth and prosperity. He's not some magic genie in the sky here to grant every wish we have. If the Lord chooses to bless you in that way, my prayer is that you steward it with open hands knowing that one day he may take it all away like he did Job, or he may tell you to sell it all like he did the rich young ruler. It's possible that he may bless you abundantly for the entirety of your life, but no matter where you stand on the spectrum, it's going to cost you greatly. In fact, it's going to cost you your life.

I didn't say it. Jesus did. He told his disciples:

Whoever wants to be my disciple must deny themselves and take up their cross and follow me. For whoever wants to save their life will lose it, but whoever loses their life for me will find it." What good will it be for someone to gain the whole world, yet forfeit their soul? Or what can anyone give in exchange for their soul? (Matthew 16:24–26)

So why do we do it? As Christ followers, have we lost our mind? I'm going to tell you right now the world thinks we have. To the world it doesn't sound fun. Don't do this. Don't do that. Check the boxes. Be good. I could go on and on, but you know exactly what I mean.

Do we do all of this to receive some reward that may be thirty, forty, fifty, sixty, or more years out? Don't get me wrong, I yearn for heaven! I yearn for the days when I get to experience the beauty and majesty of my King as I sit in his presence. The perfection. Oh, I yearn for the perfection I will get to experience in heaven. But what if there is more to this life than merely spending our whole life hoping for heaven? What if the reward isn't just years out in the future but sits right before you right now? Let's be honest, most people can't keep focused on a goal for more than a few months (think New Year's resolutions) or a few years if they are truly focused and dedicated. So how do we as humans stay focused on some reward that may be out there twenty times longer than those short three years I just mentioned—that's sixty years! Jesus prayed, "Thy kingdom come, thy will be done on earth as it is in heaven" (Matthew 6:10 KJV). He wasn't praying some empty, mindless prayer. No, he was praying that he could be the one to usher God's kingdom onto this earth. Jesus had experienced it, you know. Heaven. He has been there from before time began. He was there at creation. He is I AM!

So what do we do with all of this? How do we navigate this life knowing what I've just written above? Before we go any further, I need you to know one simple truth, so you can fully understand what this book is all about. You need to know that there's a calling on your life—that when God intricately wired your brain and gave you your skills, abilities, and gifts, he knew exactly what he was doing.

Don't second guess that!

I didn't know I had a calling until I was thirty-five years old, nearly thirty-six, but what the Lord revealed to me during that thirty-fifth year transformed my life and set me on a new journey. I was set free. The chains of bondage were no longer secured tightly around these wrists of mine. Fast-forward another four years, and I was sitting at thirty-nine almost forty. I didn't look at forty negatively as so many seem to do. I wasn't going over the hill to death. No, God had shown me the opposite—I wandered for forty years, and now I was headed over the hill into the promised land!

The message that the Lord gave me has set countless hearts and souls free as they stepped into their kingdom calling. It's time for us to break the chains of religion that grip us so tightly. It's time for us to realize that life isn't just about being good and wrapping ourselves in the sheer drudgery of avoiding the temptations of this world. No. There is more! There is life—eternal life that awaits us.

As I said above, I 100 percent believe in heaven, and one day I will be there with my heavenly Father along with a host of others. But once again here comes the juxtaposition: Jesus himself said what you're going to read next: "This is eternal life: that they know you, the only true God, and Jesus Christ, whom you have sent" (John 17:3). Eternal life starts now. You might be thinking, Okay, well, how do you know God? Jesus replied to Thomas in John 14:7 saying, "If you really know me, you will know my Father as well. From now on you do know him and have seen him." Thomas, the one who doubts, was given the key to step into eternal life that day. How? He really knew Jesus, which meant he knew the Father, which meant he stepped into eternal life right then! There is no fifty- or sixty-year wait. It's now, but it is imperative to point out that there is a quantifier in what Jesus said, so we can truly wrap our heads around the words that came out of his mouth. My wonderful mom spent her career as an English teacher turned librarian, and because of that I jokingly say all of the time that I am a word nerd. Jesus didn't just say, "If you know me." He didn't say, "If you acknowledge me." He didn't say, "If you kinda know me." No, he lays down a critical quantifier. If you *really* know me, then you know my Father as well. "This is eternal life: that they know you, the only true God, and Jesus Christ, whom you have sent."

So how do you really know Jesus? For that matter, how do you really know anyone? I'd venture to say that if you are married, you really know your spouse. You know what brings them joy. You listen to them. You know what upsets them. You spend time with them. You know your spouse inside and out, and you can tell me anything and everything I would need to know about them. Jesus is the same way. If you want to know the Father and experience eternal life, then it's time for you to *really* know the Son.

This book is the journey that led me to the BOOM. What's the BOOM? That is the purpose of this book as God orchestrated a story that I never could have made up, not in a million years. And as we go through this book, you're going to get the opportunity to see that story unfold in two parts. Part 1 is my story and my journey with the Lord. Part 2 is the revelation and application of what the Lord placed in my hands to share with you. My hope is that you read the entire book because it is jam-packed with my testimony, Scripture, and God's revelations to me as I walk this thing we like to call life.

I understand that time is one of the most precious resources we possess, especially as businesspeople. If you don't have time for part 1, please at least read chapter 8, "The Self-made Man," chapter 9, "The Voice," and all of part 2. I kept part 2 short for a reason. My prayer is that the revelation in part 2 will set you free in the same way that it set me free.

If you are not a businessperson and just happen to read this book, there are truths from my story that may also set you free. If you have no interest in business, please read part 1 and promise to read chapter 18, "The Name."

My prayer is that you recognize that this book isn't just about business as we know it, but everything about this book is about business as we know it in the kingdom of God. It's not either-or, it's always been both-and!

MEDITATIONS WITH ROSWELL

How would you define comfort? Some would contend that being uncomfortable is just simply part of the human experience…but the question is how much of our discomfort is designed by God and how much is because of our doing/ worldly dwelling? There may not be a specific "percentage," but this is a question we need to ponder/consider as we pivot from this chapter.

2

THE BUS

It was another hot, summer day—July 27, 2019 to be exact. I was stepping onto a bus that would take me to Glorieta, New Mexico, but little did I know that God had a divine appointment set up for that day. This one, though, would be between us—God and me, that is. I just didn't know it yet. One of my favorite authors, Mark Batterson, introduced me to divine appointments in his book *The Circle Maker*. I had never heard that phrase before, but since then, I have become extremely aware of those God-ordained appointments.

My church had asked me if I'd be willing to be one of the camp leaders for the third-grade boys. I jumped all over the opportunity! I'd never been to church camp before, and to top it off, my son and I would get to experience kids' camp, for the first time ever, together. I was pumped! I'm a giant kid at heart, and I love to play. But most of all I love to see the purity and innocence of kids as they enjoy the world that God created. That's how I found myself on the road to Glorieta, New Mexico, with my son, and six hundred other kids.

For four and a half hours we'd be on that bus as we made the trek from Lubbock, Texas, to New Mexico. If you've ever been to church camp, you know how it goes: big bus, lots of kids, major malfunction—it's part of the gig. Not only was the AC out, but the on-board bathroom was having some major issues. It was putting out the most rank smell my nose had ever experienced. It was as if someone lit a fire under the toilet and was cooking up something nasty that would eventually become the right side of the famous dash found on your tombstone.

There we were, forty young boys and ten men watching movies and playing games in a bus with a malfunctioning AC and bathroom. Then, to top it all off, some nasty gas was floating around. The smells were enough to knock you back in your chair. It was bad, y'all! Reflecting back, we should have called a *Survivor*-style tribal council in order to vote the worst offenders off that bus.

"Yes, ma'am, that's correct," we might have had to tell an unsuspecting mother. "One kid passed out, but we think he's going to pull through. We've never experienced anything like it, but your boy was dropping some lethal bombs on the bus, and we were extremely concerned that he was going to take some kids out. Furthermore, there were only ten adults on board, and we felt he could quite possibly take one of them out if we didn't take the necessary steps. Yes, ma'am, that is correct. Unfortunately, he was voted off the bus. It was our only option. I'm sorry. Yes, ma'am, completely off the bus. You'll have to pick him up on the side of U.S. 84 in Fort Sumner, New Mexico. Yes, ma'am. Where Billy the Kid is buried, but we gave him a Capri-Sun, a fruit snack, and some toilet paper. He's a brave little warrior, so I'm sure he'll be just fine."

Of course, that didn't happen, and all kidding aside, a conversation—no, a divine appointment—between a guy named Patrick and me was called to order. Patrick and I knew each other but not much deeper than the occasional interactions that happened when our kids played sports against one another. All I knew from those interactions is that if we ever got to spend some time together, a friendship would develop. I was sure of that.

When you've got four and a half hours on a bus, you get into things deeper than sports. You get into things deeper than what movies you enjoy. You even get into things deeper than your family. You get into life stories. God stories. You get the opportunity to share the journey that God has had you on: the peaks, the valleys, the blessings, the stories, the places where we look back and say, "Only God."

I told Patrick about the wild ride I'd been on, my time playing college football, the great moments, and then that earth-shattering moment. Yeah, that one hurt. I remember it like it was yesterday. He had some things to teach me, though—God, that is. More on that later.

I'm going to tell you the story just as I told Patrick. It leads to something big. Of course, I didn't know what was coming when I started telling my story, but God did. God had a plan for a movement, and this was the God-ordained moment to set that movement into motion—check that, more than a movement. This was a divine appointment, remember? Once you realize that God has set a divine appointment, you must be aware of every single detail. I don't want you to miss it. That divine appointment was called to be a launching pad for a culture change. It was called to wake up the body of Christ for his kingdom. This meeting was called to wake up a generation—we just didn't know it yet.

STORIES

"I don't need apologetics to prove God is real." That was a powerful statement from Terry Scalzitti, the lead pastor of Ocean View Baptist Church in South Carolina and author of the book *Parent Cue*. Terry was brought in to equip the adult leaders at the camp that weekend, and his story blew Patrick and me away. I was left speechless by what God had done in his life.

Terry was absolutely right; he didn't need science to prove God was real. All he needed was a story that only God could orchestrate. People can argue over science all day long, or they can argue over how old the earth is, but one thing they can't argue over is stories—a person's real-life experiences. Stories that no matter how hard we try, we can't make up. How can anyone dispute a real-life experience? Someone sees it. Touches it. Experiences it. It's theirs and only theirs. So what can we say against that? (See Acts 4:14 NKJV.) As we jump into this book, keep this in mind: "They triumphed over him [the devil] by the blood of the Lamb [Jesus] and by the word of their testimony [their story]; they did not love their lives so much as to shrink from death" (Revelation 12:11).

Buckle up. I've witnessed this story leave people "speechless" and give them "goosebumps." They simply can't believe what they have just heard. For that matter, I can't believe it either, but I love watching people as they process what they have just heard. I get a front row seat, and the reactions are truly something to witness. My story is one crazy, "couldn't make it up if I tried" wild ride that I hope you stick with, but here's what I need you to know more than anything—the story you're about to read, the plan that's going to be revealed throughout this book—it was never just about me.

It's always been about finding you.

MEDITATIONS WITH ROSWELL

Take a moment and reflect back to a specific time or instance when God divinely met you. Maybe it wasn't exactly a "bus" but a season of life when God showed up and revealed himself to you. Once you've identified it, rejoice, and count yourself blessed and highly favored. God has revealed himself to you!

3

THE MOMENT

Eighty-three thousand five hundred ninety-six—the official attendance that Saturday night in late November. We were under the lights at one of the decorated programs in college football: the University of Texas. And we found ourselves squaring off against the sixth ranked team in the land that night. You could tell right from the opening kick that it was gonna be a dogfight, and it didn't fail to live up to that billing. Any time you play an in-state rival, you can most certainly guarantee a fight.

We received the opening kickoff, and immediately our potent air attack went to work. It wasn't known as the Air Raid for nothing. B. J. Symons, a straight-up gunslinger, led us down the field on the opening drive for a quick score. Texas struck back quickly and then found themselves in the driver's seat for the majority of the game. Our task for the rest of the night was to battle back and keep ourselves within striking distance. We'd get down by a couple of scores and then bring it back to within one. That trend continued for most of the game until finally, with two minutes left in the game, Taurean Henderson busted through the middle of their defense and took it to the house. After battling back all game, we finally found ourselves back in the lead. The sideline went nuts. All we had to do was hold on for the remaining two minutes, and we would walk out of Austin with a road win against the sixth ranked team in the country.

Chance Mock, the backup quarterback for UT, was having no part of that. He led the Longhorns back onto the field and was able to expose a hole. Something went wrong in the secondary, and we got beat by Roy Williams for fifty-four yards, putting them deep in our territory. A few plays later, Texas connected on a nine-yard touchdown pass, and in just thirty-seven short seconds, Texas covered eighty-six yards and recaptured the lead. Once again, we found ourselves down, this time by three.

It was do or die time. With just thirty-seven seconds left in the game, we knew what we had to do. During that era of Texas Tech football, we were never out of a game. Ever. We had a never-quit attitude. We refused to lie down because we knew we could chew up yards with our Air Raid offense. After a couple of big gainers, we found ourselves on the UT side of the field. B. J. took one more shot to get a little closer, but after an incomplete pass with just three seconds left on the clock, I found myself in position to send the game into overtime.

THE KICK

As a kid I would watch SportsCenter and dream of the day that I'd have the opportunity to make the highlight reel. Here it was. As I trotted out onto the field, Dylan Gandy, one of our linemen, stopped me and told me he was praying for me as he was coming off the field. Dylan was a good friend of mine. He was a couple years older than me, but he and another teammate, Josh Rangel, led a Bible study each week at their apartment. Dylan was one of those guys you just respected and appreciated because of how he lived his life.

At forty-eight yards, it was no chip shot, but I had plenty of leg for it. Lined up seven yards behind our deep snapper, my eyes traveled up as I picked my target. You have to give yourself a mental target otherwise you're shooting blindly. As I began to take my steps back, I could hear the roar of the eighty-three-thousand-plus die-hard Longhorn fans in attendance. My job in that moment was to silence that roar and send the game into overtime. Our team had done it several times before, and I've got to tell you, there was nothing better than silencing a crowd in their own stadium. Nothing. I lined it all up, found my spot again, and began to take my two steps to the left. As I settled in, I gave one last look at my spot. My eyes came back down to my holder, Dupree, and I gave him the nod that I was ready.

Have you ever seen the movie *For Love of the Game*? Kevin Costner plays a Major League pitcher. As he prepares for each pitch, you see that he can hear all the sounds of the game, but once he's ready to zero in, he says, "Clear the mechanism." At that point, all the noise and all the distractions go away. Everything around him becomes blurry and focus kicks in. In the sports world, they call that "getting in the zone." Unlike Costner in the movie, I didn't consciously say, "Clear the mechanism," but when I settled in and nodded to Dupree, that was my brain's cue to clear the mechanism. All the noise, all the sounds—poof—they were gone. It was just me and the ball as I found myself in the zone. It went from extremely loud to complete and utter silence—all in an instant.

I crushed that ball. It felt great coming off my foot. According to Angelo Armenti in *The Physics of Sports*, college punters can achieve top launching speeds of sixty miles per hour and pros up to seventy. Placekickers achieve another ten miles per hour from running up to the ball, so college placekickers can kick around seventy miles per hour and pros around eighty. After I followed through the kick, my eyes came up to track the ball. I watched as it headed toward the uprights. "Get right! Get back right!" It definitely had the distance, but in an earth-shattering moment that ball didn't get back to the right. I missed the kick wide left. Not by much, but that doesn't matter. I missed it. I wanted it back. I wanted another shot. Whatever tiny imperfection I had as it left my foot was amplified because of the distance that imperfection had to travel.

The noise.

There was all that noise again.

It came flooding back in. This time though, it was even louder. The clock had struck 00:00. The game was over. And at just nineteen years old, as a redshirt freshman I had just experienced a life-changing, "rip your heart out and stomp on it," "punch you in the gut" moment. I squatted, took off my helmet, and put my head in my hands. I couldn't believe it. I just let my team down, and to twist the knife even deeper, it had to be against one of our in-state rivals, the University of Texas.

Mac Brown, the head coach of Texas, ran over and said something to me. I don't have a clue what he said, but knowing who he is and his character, I'm sure it was something encouraging. At that moment, though, nothing seemed to matter. Everything I had ever dreamed as a kid came to fruition. Yep, I made SportsCenter's highlight reel alright, but for all the wrong reasons. I made the front page of every sports page across the great state of Texas and beyond too. The headlines all read something like this: "Toogood not Too Good" or "Toogood No Good," and it was all settled right on top of a massive picture of me squatted down with my head in my hands.

Brutal.

The last name that everyone loves so much had found its way to the dark side. It's a double-edged sword, my last name. It's both a blessing and a curse, and it gets amplified all the more when you take on the job of a field goal kicker at the collegiate level. As a kicker, your results are either "good" or "no good," that's it. It's black and white. There is no gray area, and because of that, I had heard it all, both good and bad. It was incredibly easy for every commentator in America to have fun with my last name. This time, however, it was bad. It was really, really bad. If you are a Tech fan, I'm sorry. I can't say it enough. I let my team down, I let myself down, and I let an entire fan base down. Please know that I wanted to make that kick more than you can even imagine.

THE PATH

I got hate mail—lots of it. People talked about me behind my back—it was as real as real could get. Two guys in class the following Monday had me on absolute blast—they just had no clue I was sitting one seat in front of them. There was part of me that wanted to turn around and introduce myself. I resisted, though, and let them save face. I understood their frustration, and I also understood what came with my role as a kicker. Hero or zero. It's part of the gig.

It was a difficult time to navigate, and without a doubt, that moment would be carved into my mind for the rest of my life. The question was, what was I going to do with it? How would I respond? Here is a truth we can put all our hope in. When the world turns its back on you, God will be there to wrap you up in his arms. Did you catch that? Read that last sentence again. When the world turns its back on you, God will be there to wrap you up in his arms and fill you with peace, understanding, and absolute certainty during times of absolute uncertainty. In God's Word Paul wrote, "And the peace of God, which surpasses all understanding, will guard your hearts and your minds in Christ Jesus" (Philippians 4:7 ESV). If you get nothing out of this chapter, please take that away. As any loving father would do, God took that moment and began to teach me. He put me on a new path. A path that would free me. A path that would direct me to new understandings. A path that would undoubtedly shape the rest of my life. He began the long and difficult process of breaking down my need to please people, my dependence on my works, and in my ability to be "good" instead of where it should have been all along—in him. I've got many more defining moments I could point to in my life, even during my career at Tech, but none can compare to that one. All of those moments, every single one, were instrumental in leading me to a deeper relationship with God. But through that one, he wanted to reveal a new path. A better path. A freeing path. He was taking me off that nasty path of always telling myself I had to keep everyone happy, and he immediately put me on the path of pleasing the only one that mattered—him.

Can I tell you something about people-pleasing? If you identify as a people pleaser, listen to this. Please, I'm begging you, listen to this. You will undoubtedly please people, and if you get lucky, and it's the people you want to please, it will feel great. It will fill you up, and a small drip of endorphins will run through your body—but only for a moment. That feeling will vanish as quickly as it showed up when you meet someone else you think needs to be pleased. Beware! This is the ugly, ugly side of being a people pleaser. No matter how hard you try, the moment you please someone or some group of people, you will most certainly displease someone else or another group of people simultaneously. You cannot keep everyone happy. Let me say it another way. You cannot keep everyone happy. See what I did there? There is no other way around it. No matter your intentions, and how well you may do something, someone will find a fault. It's inevitable. My hope is that everyone who reads this book loves it, but I can't hang my hat on that. I know that's not likely. I can't put my hope in pleasing everyone, and you can't either. You will come to the end of a very long and difficult road and find yourself flat-out exhausted. And to top it off, you will have very little to show for it. It's an exhausting, unending game. Let me just go ahead and break it to you: it's a game you can never win and a kick you'll always miss wide left.

No one wants to be that guy who misses the game-tying kick. I didn't want to be that guy, the goat—and I'm not talking a Michael Jordan type of GOAT (Greatest of All Time). I'm talking about the goat that gets blamed for some sort of unfortunate thing that transpires in life. That goat. The reality is we don't know when, or how, those moments are going to come. Sometimes those life-altering moments are private and sometimes they are public, but one thing is certain. They will create an opportunity to learn and grow. Mine was extremely public, but even in the most humiliating public crash I could imagine at that time, God immediately went to work and began to pick up the pieces and shape me through that difficult and challenging moment.

The president of my high school, Dr. Vaughn Luster, always said, "You can get bitter, or you can get better." I'm pretty sure he wasn't the one to coin that saying, but the deeper I dug, the more I began to unearth a little golden nugget buried inside of it. When I looked at the word *bitter*, and I looked at the word *better*, there was but one simple letter that separated the two—the letter *i*. So now I say it like this, "You can get bitter, or you can get better. And the only difference between those two words is the letter *i*. I have the choice, and the same can be said for you." That little quote can help change your perspective from that of a victim to that of an overcomer. From feeling sorry for yourself to rising up. From getting down on yourself to a pivot. When a moment comes along that devastates every fiber inside of you, will you get bitter or will you get better?

THE REMEDY

Now let's get real. Not a single one of us likes to talk about our failures, our shortcomings, and all the epic ways we fell flat on our face. No one. Not one of us. We put on that perfect mask and hide behind the good times, never to reveal where we fell. Or where we fail. People have told me, "You shouldn't talk about that kick. You need to move on." They think I haven't healed from it. They think I'm still beating myself up over that kick. It's actually 100 percent the opposite. When your faith is rooted in God Almighty, the King of kings, the Lord of lords, the God of the angel armies, and you decide to put all your trust in him, you begin to see his hand in each and every situation you find yourself in no matter how bad it may have been. I'll say it all day every day and scream it from the rooftops: my greatest desire in the world was to make that kick. But I didn't. That's the reality, and I can't change that. As much as I wish I could, I can't get in Doc Brown's DeLorean, go back in time, and rewrite history. But here is the beauty in that kick: it doesn't define me, and your failures or missteps don't define you. The devil wants both of us to believe that is the case, that we are failures. He worked hard for it to define me. He wants your failures to define you, but here is the deal: failure is not a person. That's what the devil wants you to believe. The truth is, it's a thing, an event, a moment in time, but never, I repeat, never, a person! That missed kick—an event, a moment in time—became an integral part of my testimony. You heard that right. God picked up those shattered and broken pieces of my heart and soul and began to shape me into who he desired for me to become through that missed kick.

Way back in the Old Testament there's a story of a boy named Joseph who found himself sold into slavery by his own flesh and blood, accused of making sexual advances toward his master's wife, and trapped behind the cold bars of a prison cell, all contrary to the dreams he had when he was just a teenager. You see, when he was seventeen, Joseph had had some vivid, prophetic dreams from God, foretelling great things for his life. So how can that be if he is rotting in a cold, dark prison for something he didn't even do? Joseph knew that God had bigger plans for his life than siting in that gloomy cell. In fact, Scripture gives us a glimpse into Joseph's psyche at that time. After interpreting a dream the cup bearer had, Joseph looked him directly in the eye and said, "But when all goes well with you, remember me and show me kindness; mention me to Pharaoh and get me out of this prison. I was forcibly carried off from the land of the Hebrews, and even here I have done nothing to deserve being put in a dungeon" (Genesis 40:14–15). In other words, "I'm not supposed to be here! God had a plan for my life, and he revealed that plan through the dreams I had as a young boy. I've got to get out of here. There is no way God's plan for my life can be accomplished while I'm trapped in this prison. This nasty dungeon is not where I'm supposed to be! God had a plan!" Then tragedy strikes again; the cup bearer forgot—or maybe he didn't care—but in a devastating turn of events, Joseph remained in that prison for two more years!

Now here is something I don't want you to miss. Through all of the twists and turns that occurred in Joseph's life, he maintained his trust in the Lord. Deep down, he knew he was not supposed to be in that prison, and that there was more that God would do with his life, but he patiently waited for God to work. What his brothers meant for harm, God was about to flip it all upside down and undoubtedly work it for good. Joseph's remedy: the Lord God Almighty! As I read the account of Joseph, five words leapt off the pages of Scripture and became a common theme in his life: "The Lord was with Joseph." "Through it all the LORD was with Joseph so that he prospered. . . . The LORD was with him; he showed him kindness and granted him favor in the eyes of the prison warden. . . . The LORD was with Joseph and gave him success in whatever he did" (Genesis 39:2, 21, 23). **The Lord was with Joseph!** So when his brothers showed up on the scene, and God fulfilled the dreams that Joseph had as a young boy, he was so overcome that the Bible tells us he wept. Twenty-three years had passed, and Joseph was now a forty-year-old man who wept and sobbed uncontrollably. I imagine he wept as his entire life flashed before his eyes as he marveled at the goodness and faithfulness of God. I imagine he wept as the realization came that God saved his people, the Israelites, through the tumultuous, difficult road he had to walk. I imagine he wept as the realization that his life was not his own clearly came into focus—the realization that his brothers didn't do this to him. No! God orchestrated every bit of it as he went before Joseph into this foreign land. He wept because he saw the magnitude of how great and how mighty God truly was to him way back then, and I declare still is to us today.

God was Joseph's remedy, and he is our remedy today. Allow him to lead you through the valleys and the tumultuous, difficult times of this life. Because when you do, you may stand on the other side overcome with emotion and weep as God's goodness shines through the darkest moments of your life.

My story just doesn't have the same kick without that kick. That horrific moment led me to a godly pivot, a pivot that would allow God to wrap you up in the pages of this book. So far you have gotten to see just one set of the cards that I had been dealt. That set of cards with the kick quite frankly sucked. I was faced with a decision to make, and as I write this, I marvel at all the decisions and challenges we face in this life. It's a daily journey—a daily battle. And because of that, we must be open to God's direction as he leads us to a deeper understanding of who he created us to be.

We live in a fallen world, and because of that, you'll undoubtedly experience pain in this life. Maybe you won't be sold into slavery and thrown in prison like Joseph, or miss a kick in front of 83,596 people in attendance and a bunch more watching on TV, but take note, there will be something. Big or small, you will experience some sort of failure and plenty of pain in this life. It's a part of the human condition.

Jesus revealed the gift of the Holy Spirit to the disciples and the promise and access that he will bring. He disclosed the pains we will experience in this life, but he immediately gave them hope with a promise of joy—a joy that can be found only in him (see John 16:16). And as you get to the end of the chapter, Jesus ties it all together: "I have told you these things, so that in me you may have peace. In this world you will have trouble. But take heart! I have overcome the world" (John 16:33).

What an incredible promise! What a gift! We will experience trouble, there is no doubt about it, but his promise stands! He has overcome the world! As you take that in, please allow yourself to rest in that truth. And the next time you line up a kick and miss it wide left…do yourself a favor.

Seek the remedy.

MEDITATIONS WITH ROSWELL

Sometimes in life we experience things that don't make sense. Maybe everything you've worked for your entire life is seemingly compromised or ruined, and for what?

After reading this chapter, there may be a thousand thoughts running through your mind, but know this: God turns pain into joy, creates beauty from ashes and in many ways, beautifully ruins our lives to produce a greater and more fulfilled future.

4

THE CAREER

Up and down. Those would be the words I would use to describe the rest of my career at Texas Tech. Injuries, and me losing my sole, seemed to be the proverbial thorn in my flesh. You'd think after that missed kick in Austin, I'd have learned that God wanted me on a different path, one of pleasing only him, but that weed of wanting to do things my way had some incredibly deep roots. It wasn't going to be a simple tug to remove that deeply rooted, prideful weed. It was going to take a shovel—no, a backhoe to remove that bad boy.

2004

Our 2004 season opened up in Dallas against SMU. I grew up in Rowlett, Texas, which was just fifteen minutes east of downtown Dallas, so that game was like a homecoming for me. Over fifty of my family and friends were in attendance that day, which normally would make a guy feel great, but no one knew I had a sprain in my plant foot ankle that was in pretty rough shape. I had been getting treatment, and I felt like it was one of those things I could play through, but I was wrong. I went out for my first field goal on the opening drive and just couldn't sit down on my left leg. I pushed that kick wide right. On our next possession, we'd roll in for our first touchdown of the season, taking the lead 6-3. I ran out for the extra point, but the same thing happened. I couldn't get the torque I needed on my plant leg and committed about the worst sin a kicker can commit. I missed the extra point. At that point the coaches were furious, and I quickly found myself on the bench for the remainder of the game. As the clock hit zero, we had won the game 27-13, but my job as the starting field goal kicker was shot. I spent the next week in a walking boot, and after getting some treatment and rest I was able to come back for the third game of the season against TCU. I would start handling the kickoff duties from that point on as Alex Trlica, who had a cannon for a leg and ice in his veins, was doing a great job on field goals after taking my place. I was just grateful to have another shot to be on the field and for the opportunity to help our team in any way I could. The 2004 season was one I'll always remember. It ended with us blasting the fifth ranked California Golden Bears, led by Aaron Rogers, in the Holiday Bowl. We whupped them boys 45-31.

2005

Starting my junior year, I again found myself with the starting kickoff job. I loved kickoff! The energy in the stadium was hyped up, and if I didn't put one through the end zone for a touchback, there was always the chance I might get to hit someone. No one wanted to be the guy who got tackled by the kicker, so it was always a blast to come downhill on a returner.

September 10, 2005: Florida International. As pregame warm-ups were wrapping up, I felt the need to get one more kickoff in before we headed to the locker room, so I took my approach and sent one more kick into the north end zone, but something just wasn't right. I looked down, and the sole of my shoe had completely ripped off. That of course is no small thing, but it shouldn't have been cause for concern.

We were sponsored by Nike, so I ran over to our equipment manager and let him know I needed another shoe. It went something like this.

"Jeff! Hey, Jeff! I need another shoe, man. My shoe just blew out." I held it up for him to see the sole of my shoe hanging on by a thread.

"What size do you need?

"It's a 12."

"We don't have any that size."

"What?" We are sponsored by Nike. What do you mean we don't have any that size?"

"We're out. We don't even have any close to that size. We've possibly got the old style if you want that."

"Alright, get me what you've got. I just need a shoe!"

This is the best way I can relate what happened with that shoe: it'd be like you teeing off on the first nine holes and blasting drive after drive down the middle of the fairway. Your friends, seeing how you are absolutely crushing the ball, keep giving you high fives and telling you what a great game of golf you are playing that day. You're feeling pretty good after an amazing front nine as you make the turn and get ready to replicate what just happened on the back nine. Just as you tee up on the tenth hole, one of your friends stops you and pushes your ball and tee closer to the ground. You take your swing, but instead of blasting it down the middle of the fairway like you did on the front nine, it's by far your worst shot of the day. You top the ball so bad that it doesn't at all go where you wanted, and that drive leaves you in a terrible position for your next shot. That's in essence what happened when my shoe blew up.

It was time for the opening kick, and the coin flip determined we would open the game on defense, which meant we'd be kicking off. I didn't get any kicks in with that new shoe, but I wasn't too concerned. I thought I'd be alright, until I wasn't. The sole of these new shoes was thicker, which basically made me just a little taller. And when it comes to kicking, millimeters matter.

The stadium was hyped. The drum line was gettin' it. The atmosphere was electric until I sucked all of the life out of it with one swing of my leg. My opening kickoff went out of bounds, and we were assessed a fifteen-yard penalty on the very first play of the season. I singlehandedly took all the air and excitement out of that stadium. It was like a bad drive off the tee box. The coaches were upset but understanding, until the second kickoff. The second ball took the same path as it sailed out of bounds. I quickly found myself on the same bench that kept me warm in early 2004, but this time it became a permanent home for me. I was planted there for the remainder of the year. As the years have passed, I look back at that moment and have found quite a bit of irony from that day. Check this out. The sole of my shoe was ripped off that day so that the soul of my life could be ripped wide open.

When it came to football, my junior season was a complete bust. I felt as though God was slamming the door shut on my dreams of playing football in college and the NFL, so I began the process of making a game plan for the rest of my life. At that point, I already had a degree in marketing, so I seriously contemplated quitting at the end of the season. I thought, *What's the point?* I considered transferring to West Texas A&M, but that didn't seem like something I would truly enjoy. I was confused, and one thing was certain: a bout of depression had overcome me, and I didn't know what to do. My dreams, my identity, everything that gave me worth was gone like a vapor dissipating into thin air.

My girlfriend at the time, who is now my rock star of a wife, was talking to me about all of it. Brandi said, "Don't quit. You may not be starting anymore, but God has something for you. You are called to be a light in that locker room, and I promise God will do something with that." I know for all you men that this will be a complete shocker, but she was right. Aren't they always, though? God had planted me in that locker room to be a difference maker, but deep down it was hard for me to come to terms with that potential reality. I wanted to be on that field. I'm a competitor, and I had a dream to pursue, after all. Regardless of my own personal situation, our 2005 season was a blast and turned out to be a great year. We finished the season with a 9-3 record after we lost to Alabama by three in the Cotton Bowl. And if you have ever watched that game, I want to go on the record. His knee was definitely down.

So here comes my senior year, and I had zero expectations of finding my way back onto the field. Zero. Zilch. Nada. I'd come to grips with the fact that my career hadn't gone as I would have planned, but I was enjoying the camaraderie of the locker room that spring and summer. I was getting to hang with my boys every day, and there wasn't much better than that.

As I headed into the summer of 2006, life was changing. Something new was being born, and my spirit was stirring as God got a hold of me like I had never experienced before. I was a guy who hated to read. I've always said that was my "rebellion." I know, big rebellion, right? You see, my mom was a librarian at the local middle school, so I would give every excuse in the book on why I didn't read. "It makes my neck hurt." "It makes me tired." "It's so boring." "I don't get anything out of it." I'd do anything, and I mean anything, to get out of reading. I hated it. Yet God began to transform me, and I found I just couldn't put a book down. He was having me do something I had never done before as I went from a guy who never picked a book up to a guy who never put a book down. I wish I could remember all the books I read that summer, but one that really hit home was *The Purpose Driven Life* by Rick Warren. I stopped watching TV. I stopped playing video games. I did nothing that summer but read. In a massive turn of events, God had finally broke me of people-pleasing. He broke me of my self-righteous pride and revealed that being good and performing for others was not all there was in this life. He showed me that it was all about him. He introduced me to what a relationship with him looked like as he ripped out that deeply rooted, prideful, religious spirit.

My soul was set on fire as the spirit of a dead man walking was plucked out and destroyed. You see, I was the epitome of the living, breathing dead. Prior to this personal awakening, I was stuck in religion, which was exactly where the devil wanted me to be. All the while, though, God continued to dig—to pluck—to uproot as he moved me away from religion and into his greatest desire with us—relationship. There were many painful moments along the way. Being refined by fire is never easy, but with plenty of heat and a backhoe he finally got deep enough to yank that nasty, deeply rooted religious spirit out from within me. I had felt the initial tug three years prior, and I had seen some change throughout those three years that preceded this one, but it was slow and methodical. I'll be the first to admit that I am quite hardheaded, so he took the one thing I found all my value in—football—and ripped it away for a season. God was challenging me to go deeper with him. He was challenging me to experience him in a way I never had. He wanted more.

Oh, by the way, I find it amazing, and really quite comical, that God would take a guy who absolutely hated to read, flip him upside down, and have him write books that encourage you to read. Who knew? God did!

2006: A FRESH START

Suddenly, I found myself back on the field. But instead of worrying about what everyone thought, and praying I would perform so people would be pleased with me, my prayer became this: "Heavenly Father, let me go out and represent you on this field. God, I pray that any applause that comes down for what I do would be reflected off of me and directed back to you." I prayed that prayer every single time I ran on that field. I wanted to please my heavenly Father. Nothing else mattered anymore. What truly mattered was using the talent he gave me to advance his kingdom.

Man, that senior season looked different. Not only did I find myself kicking off again, but God set me up to be one of the spiritual leaders on the team. I was asked to lead the prayer in the locker room for a group of guys before every game, and as we'd get to the end zone after running out on the field, I'd lead the team in prayer there as well. God even went beyond the walls of that locker room and expanded my influence in other areas. I was asked to speak at FCA events, a local church, and at various other events. They wanted me to share my story. Not only was my influence in the locker room and off the field growing, but my performance on the field was the best it had been since starting my career at Tech. Kickoffs were flying out the back of the end zone as I did everything I could to help set our defense up for success. One of my favorite coaches, Ruffin McNeil (Coach Ruff), always told us in that booming, grizzly voice of his, "Kickoff is the first play of defense, so set them up for success!" That was my job, and I was doing it well.

In a crazy turn of events, I went from sitting the bench my junior year to leading the Big 12 in touchbacks and finishing third in the country in touchbacks my senior year. Incredibly, I was able to accomplish all of that while missing three games due to contracting mono in the latter half of the season. It was an amazing time and an incredible gift that God gave me during that 2006 season. Once it all came to an end, I had garnered the attention of agents and NFL scouts. My dream of the NFL was alive and well once again. In just one short year, I had gone from thinking my career was over to having an agent represent me, receiving offers to work out in front of NFL scouts, and an opportunity to pursue my childhood dream. Only God could do that; he flipped the script!

REFINED

None of it was easy. I had to go through the refinery. I had to be broken down. It was imperative that if I wanted to understand God's plan, I had to get reworked, and I had to get reshaped. If I've learned anything during this life, it's that we don't always understand the journey. We don't always understand why certain things happen in our life, but let me tell you, God has a plan. God began to show me what life looks like when we begin to depend on him. He began to show me that it isn't about pursuing our dream or our passion and occasionally giving him a nod of approval along the way. It's actually quite the opposite. It's about pursuing his dreams and his passions for your life all while trying to keep pace with him along the way. He has a dream for your life. He has a plan much greater than any dream you could imagine on your own, but it takes dying to yourself. It takes dying to your agenda and being born again (see John 3:3). You are designed to be a kingdom warrior, one who advances the kingdom because you have made the decision to go all out, dive deep, and give everything you've got to the King of kings as you pursue the dreams he has for your life.

Check it out. Listen carefully to this. Dying to yourself is the hardest thing we can do. The fact is, we are born into a sinful nature, and part of that sinful nature is rooted in self-ishness—a selfishness that teaches us to fight for ourselves. A selfishness that has turned us into a society that reeks of "me-ness." A society that screams at the top of our lungs, "Look at me! Look at me! I matter! I'm important too!" Just look at social media. Need I say more?

In one of my favorite books in the Bible, Galatians, Paul drops a bomb on the people of Galatia as he addresses their bend toward a sinful, selfish desire. I don't always love the Message version of the Bible, but I do in Galatians 5. I love the depth the translator uses to get Paul's point across when he says:

> My counsel is this: Live freely, animated and motivated by God's Spirit. Then you won't feed the compulsions of selfishness. For there is a root of sinful self-interest in us that is at odds with a free spirit, just as the free spirit is incompatible with selfishness. These two ways of life are antithetical, so that you cannot live at times one way and at times another way according to how you feel on any give day. Why don't you choose to be led by the Spirit and so escape the erratic compulsions of a law-dominated existence? (Galatians 5:16–18 MSG)

Paul is drawing a line in the sand. Quit giving into the sinful nature that is rooted in what's best for me and instead pursue the life of freedom that is motivated by God's Spirit! It is a freedom that can be found only in Christ and is incompatible with a selfishness rooted in the devil. They can't co-exist. You must ditch one to pursue the other. But beware, the devil can warp your thinking into believing that your pursuit (rooted in selfishness) is God's plan for your life. You must ask yourself, "Does this advance my kingdom and agenda, or does it advance God's kingdom and agenda?"

It's time to die to our own selfish agenda—crucify it for good. It's time to let Jesus' blood truly redeem us and live in the freedom that can only be found in him. It's time to get on God's plan—to experience something new—something fresh—something kingdom. Will you get off that old cycle, die to yourself, and let God do the work of excavating that deeply rooted selfishness? Will you allow him to cultivate his desires for your life? Will you allow him to yank out a religious spirit and set you free to live out your kingdom calling?

The choice is yours.

~

MEDITATIONS WITH ROSWELL

Take as much time as you need and consider your own career: the ups, the downs, the twists, and the turns. Now answer this: Is it worth it to die to yourself and allow God to renovate you? Do you truly believe he makes all things new? I'll leave you with these words of Jesus: "Most assuredly, I say to you, unless a grain of wheat falls into the ground and dies, it remains alone; but if it dies, it produces much grain" (John 12:24 NKJV).

5

THE CURSOR

"I didn't need you in the NFL at that time." Those words bounced back and forth over and over as they echoed in my mind. *Overwhelmed,* that's the best word I can use to describe that moment as those ten simple words stopped me dead in my tracks and brought tears to my eyes. In that moment, on February 7, 2020, almost thirteen years since my football career ended, God, through the Holy Spirit, absolutely crushed me with those words. After all those years, I finally got an answer to the biggest question I had in the back of my mind. That twelve-year eight-month gap was never easy. It presented new challenges—things I never would have predicted. It's as if my life had started completely over. A reboot.

Start>Windows>Power>Restart: "Please shut down all other programs to successfully restart your life." "In order to restart, you must close the following programs that are open. Are you sure you want to proceed?" The cursor flashes at you. Fear of the unknown comes rushing in. The work I've done—will I lose it all? The computer asks you if you want to close the programs. The cursor keeps flashing. Waiting. You almost feel as though it's taunting you. You weigh the risk as you consider the power that one little button holds. Complete deconstruction of everything you had known and worked toward now meets you face to face. Two options are all you get: OK and cancel. That's it. You think to yourself,

"Is there any way around this? Is there any way to restart but keep this one program open? There has to be another way!" The cursor—it keeps flashing. Waiting.

THE BIG BUCKS

Two hundred bucks a game—fifty more if we won. I could earn up to a thousand bucks a month. It was lucrative. In fact, it was so lucrative that I got another job waiting tables at Texas Roadhouse. Those big bucks were what we got paid when I kicked in the Arena Football's developmental league (AF2). Since I hadn't kicked field goals in a while, my coach felt it'd be a good idea to get some live kicks in while getting the opportunity to stay fresh at the same time. That league fell between the end of my senior season and the beginning of what I hoped would be my rookie year. I thought that was a great idea, so off I went to play for the Lubbock Renegades and then Oklahoma City Yard Dawgz. I don't care who you are, the spelling of Dawgz alone is enough to get you hyped up.

I gave it a go. I gave it all I had. I got invited in for a workout with the Bills and Cowboys, but that door to the NFL never fully opened. I was confused. I didn't understand. I asked God, "Why would you rip it all away my junior year, give it back my senior year with a clear mission to make an impact in the locker rooms, only to slam the door in my face once again nine months later? It doesn't make sense. I feel like you played me. I don't even know what else I'm good at. Now what do I do?"

Can you relate? The time had come. The cursor—it was God—flashing. Waiting. He was ready to start the next chapter. I had bone spurs in my back, a compressed disc, and a pulled hamstring. Then there were the odds. Let's get into that for just a minute. I'm a numbers guy, so I started to calculate the odds of making an NFL roster. Most teams carry only one kicker. Back then, two guys could make the squad if there was a kickoff specialist, but the reality was the league was loaded with veteran kickers. There are thirty-two NFL teams, and I bet about twenty-nine of those teams all had a veteran. So I had to be one of three in the world. One of three in the world. Let that sink in for just a moment. I needed to ask myself some serious questions. How long do I pursue this? God, what is it that you desire out of my life? Is this worth it? I had a beautiful wife back home, and together, we had agreed to give this a shot, but I missed her. Life just wasn't the same without her. We had been married only two short months when we made the decision for me to move to Oklahoma City and for her to stay back in Lubbock to finish school. As a man, I am called to provide and protect, and I didn't feel like I was upholding my end of the deal. The cursor was flashing, waiting. The time had come. I had to ask myself, Am I really ready to click that button? God was ready, but I wasn't sure if I was. Then in one of the most difficult moments of my life, I pushed the button and chose to restart. The inevitable was here. The time had come to hang 'em up.

Why do you do what you do, God? I was positive I knew what you wanted out of my life. Why did you close that door?

Can we take a moment and establish something right here, right now? If you get nothing out of this book, I want this one statement to be clear. God knows better. Better than me. Better than you. Better than anyone you may get advice from. God knows better. And if you're willing to submit to his authority, and trust that he has a well-documented, well-orchestrated masterful set of plans written for your life, then once you fully understand that truth, you will be able to weather the ups, the downs, the kicks that go wide left, and keep your eyes locked on him. We need to get past acknowledging him. Our society is great at that. It's great at that nod of approval. But he doesn't just want to be acknowledged. He's not looking for a shout out here or there. He wants to be obeyed. He wants you to abide in him. And when you abide in him, he finally gets the opportunity to take you on the ride of a lifetime. A ride that will undoubtedly lead to freedom. Stop right here for a moment, grab your Bible or Bible app and read John 15:5–17 in the New King James Version. Go ahead, I'll wait right here.

Abide in him, obey his promptings, and watch in awe as God creates an undeniable story in your life as he places you at the epicenter of the BOOM!

It's here. The time is right. Now is the time to ask this question. Why are we so insistent on ruling our own life? Why do we dig our heels into the ground and think we know better? As men, we all want to have influence. We all are born with the desire for kingship. It's innately born in us—that kingship. We play king of the jungle. We fight and wrestle to see who will be king of the mountain. But we get ourselves into trouble when we declare that we are the ultimate king. Why do we rail against God so hard and insist on being the ultimate king? The truth is, we aren't wrong. We are, in fact, all kings. The apostle Peter said we are a royal priesthood (1 Peter 2:9). But I've got news for you. You better not allow yourself to get too big for your britches because we serve the King of kings. Notice the capital *K* and the little *k*. Don't get it twisted. That's not just for ancient biblical times. "The word of God is alive and active. Sharper than any double-edged sword, it penetrates even to dividing soul and spirit, joints and marrow; it judges the thoughts and attitudes of the heart" (Hebrews 4:12). It was written for you, and it was written for me. We need to remember our place. It's time for us to step in line with the true and ultimate King. As my kicking career came to an end, I packed my bags and headed back to Lubbock, Texas, having no clue what my future would hold.

A NEW CHALLENGE

"What do you want to do?" I was twenty-three years old and had no clue what I wanted to do with my life when my Brandi asked me that question. I started mowing lawns when I was nine years old and continued that through college, but as I sat there with my wife, I just couldn't see that as a lifelong career path at the time. My roommate from college and I had done some video editing as a side hustle. I enjoyed that quite a bit, so I guess that could be a viable option. I did have a degree in marketing, and I did have that internship from the summer of 2005 when I worked for a local marketing firm. My video editing experience came into play there as they put me with the department that made commercials for local businesses, but I didn't like sitting in front of a computer all day long. I'm more of a busybody, so in all reality, marketing or video editing as a profession would probably not be the best fit for me. And that's pretty much all I knew—sports, mowing, and video editing. Now what?

I took one of those career assessment tests. Near the top of the list came restaurant management. I enjoyed those couple of months waiting tables at Texas Roadhouse in Oklahoma City, but other than that I had no restaurant experience. I had degrees in marketing, management, and general business, so maybe I was equipped to step into a career path in the hospitality business. I wasn't sure, though, so I asked my father-in-law for advice. My father-in-law is a tremendously successful businessman, but of course that success didn't just come easy. He worked hard for years, and I'm sure he had some sleepless nights to get where he is. But one of the things that makes him a great leader is his ability to operate as a team player. He wants others to experience great success as well, so as the one charged to carry out the God-given vision of his business, he sees beyond what stands before him each day. He sees the opportunity for success out on the horizon and acts upon it. The thing I love about him and how he operates his business is that he doesn't just hoard all that success to himself. He wants to take his entire team with him. Occasionally though, he has those moments where not everyone can grasp the vision. Not everyone can see beyond what stands in front of them day to day, so there are times where he has to sit down with someone and ask the simple question: "Why do I have to drag you to success?" He then takes that question to another level as he gives them more to think about. "If there was a bus to guaranteed success sitting outside, and I offered you a ticket, would you get on it? And once you got on, would you be happy just for yourself, or would you sit by the bus driver and give him addresses of other people you want to take with you? Why must you kick and scream and dig your heels into the ground when I try and get you on that bus? Why do I have to drag you to success?" My father-in-law and his family have deep roots in the restaurant business. He followed in the footsteps of his dad and uncles and became a Pizza Hut franchisee in the eighties. Then in 1996, while still operating the Huts, he bought the rights in Lubbock and Eastern New Mexico to a west Texas staple, Taco Villa. If you're ever in Lubbock, Texas, you've got to hit up a Taco Villa. People go nuts over that place.

After discussing his company, and the opportunities that were available, he offered me a job. So in July 2007, Brandi and I packed our bags and headed to Plainview, Texas, population 21,693. I started my career in the restaurant business as a mid-level assistant manager at the local Pizza Hut. As any new job goes, it took some adjusting, but once I got in the groove of things, I definitely enjoyed the business. Now, please don't jump to conclusions and think this was some sort of free ride. It was the exact opposite. He treated me just as he was treated, and I appreciated that. He values hard work, diligence, and a full understanding of the operation. You must understand every detail inside the business in order to run it with the precision that it is owed. He has high expectations, and those expectations make his company what it is today. You aren't given franchisee of the year awards by Pizza Hut for nothing.

As the years passed, I took on various roles within the company. I started as an assistant manager and then became restaurant manager and then general manager and then area manager overseeing multiple locations.

DREAMS

In 2011 an opportunity presented itself. My father-in-law had been working on a new restaurant concept, and I was going to help launch and develop that brand. This one would be located in the Austin, Texas, area, Round Rock, to be exact. So once again my gracious and very pregnant wife and I, along with our fourteen-month-old son, packed our bags and made the 350-mile trip to Cedar Park, Texas. This would be the fifth place in just four years of marriage we would call home. We were moving pros by that point, and quite frankly, we were willing to do whatever it took to make our dreams come true. As we prepared for that move, the search for a new home was in order. We were ready to put some roots down and find a place we could call home, possibly for the rest of our lives. We met with our realtor, and on the first weekend of scouting out homes, Brandi and I found our dream home.

It was a new construction home that had everything we could ever want. It had four bedrooms and a little bonus room where the kids could play, and it fit into our monthly budget. Not only that, but we got in early enough to make selections for the house. Brandi is incredibly talented at interior design, and she sees color and space better than anyone I've ever met. So we left that weekend feeling pretty good about that house and the opportunity that lay ahead.

As we got closer to closing on that house, something was off. After going under contract, I got a funny feeling in my gut. I felt like something was saying not to buy that house. Maybe it was just my nerves. After all, it was the biggest purchase we had ever made up to that point in our lives, so maybe I was getting cold feet. I didn't know how to reconcile those feelings, so I sought out wisdom from family and close friends whom I respected. They reminded me that the bank had pre-approved us, and my father-in-law offered a bonus in exchange for the sweat equity we would put in to getting the brand successfully launched. Once I remembered that, and ran those numbers in my head, I felt quite a bit better. After all, we could afford it on my salary alone, so we proceeded with the purchase of that home, and hit the road to Cedar Park, Texas.

As we made the move, Brandi and I were even more excited to be welcoming our second child in the coming months. This time though, it would be a sweet baby girl that we would get to bring home to that new house. Man, we loved that house. Laughter filled the rooms. New friendships commenced. Memories and dreams were birthed in that house—dreams that would change the course of our family's future. As we settled into that new home, I got to work on developing the business and doing everything I could to build a brand. By all accounts, the all-American dream was right in front of us.

We could see it. We could taste it. We could touch it. A beautiful family, an awesome house in the suburbs of one of the fastest growing metros in America, and a business that had unlimited potential. By all accounts, it was everything I could have dreamed of. I was twenty-eight years old, and the future looked incredibly bright. Our very own American dream was unfolding right before our very eyes.

Until it wasn't.

We couldn't see it—the storm, that is. It was brewing and angrily loomed up ahead. It was developing beyond my vision and would lead to yet another one of those defining moments in my life—an altar-building moment. A place I could go back to time and time again when I need a reminder of God's prompting, his provision, his leading. That cursor.

The cursor flashes. It waits patiently. It's ready to author and pen the most incredible story you could ever imagine. One that you could never make up—not even if you were the most creative person in the world. Why? Because even if you had the title of most creative person in the world, there is still one that is greater than you. The Creator is the one with the pen. The one we talked about earlier, the King of kings—the one with the capital *K*—yeah, that one. He's the one holding the pen so that leaves just one last question:

Will you click yes?

MEDITATIONS WITH ROSWELL

Have you ever deeply considered that God is the author or blinking cursor that is waiting for you to humbly and obediently submit to his plan? For so many of us, there are countless programs in our lives that need to be shut down. What might that be for you? Are you willing to click yes?

6

THE STORM

It came in like a tsunami, barreling toward the shore. I wasn't expecting a storm that day, so I definitely wasn't prepared for the magnitude and the power of those waves as they surrounded me. After the first wave came crashing in, the second wave came barreling in mere seconds behind the first. As I experienced the power of those waves, I was instantly overcome by a sense of awe and wonder, but to my surprise, I didn't turn in fear and run for higher grounds. Rather, I stood there confidently anchored into the one Rock that my feet had found. The power of those waves was undeniable. The first wave was a total shock. The second one, however, refreshed me. The waves were speaking to me, and as I began to process the information, the message I received filled every nook and cranny of available space in my mind. In an instant, everything else vanished—gone. I could think of nothing else as those two waves echoed back and forth. It was all I could hear.

A SHIFT IN THE WIND

It was another beautiful morning in Cedar Park, Texas—a suburb that sits just northwest of Austin. It was Thursday, March 7, 2013, to be exact. As I got in my truck, the sun was out, the air was crisp, and we were headed toward another day in the lower seventies. But as I drove my son to mother's day out, there was a heaviness pressing in on me. The storm was no longer beyond the horizon. It was here. It was now. And it wasn't letting up. We found ourselves smack-dab in the middle of a raging storm that had been brewing for eighteen months. The excitement of the new house and the American dream had turned into anxiety, fear, and uncertainty. With the addition of our daughter, expenses had gone up, but my income had not. There was no bottom line. There was no bonus coming in. It wasn't due to a lack of effort or execution; the new restaurant concept just wasn't taking hold. We had done anything and everything we could to drum up business. We dropped coupons, worked with nearby schools, set up catering deals with local churches. You name it, we tried it, but nothing seemed to work. And once again, I found myself asking the same question I had asked before. "Why, God? I don't understand what you are doing. Why'd you move us five hours from everything we knew, rip us away from family, and allow these difficult circumstances to come our way, all for this? More debt, less giving, and a whole bunch of anxiety?"

More uncertainty.

More questions.

More confusion.

As my son sat in the backseat, anchored down by his five-point harness, the twenty-minute trek to his mother's day out program gave me some time to reflect on life and pray. At that point, reflection looked more like desperation, and prayer became quite a bit more frequent. Once again, I had no clue what was going on with my life. Another storm. Another difficult circumstance. *Will I ever catch a break?*

From the outside looking in, everything appeared perfect, but the inside was full of nothing but uncertainty and doubt, doubt about whether I was doing what I was supposed to be doing with my life. Doubt about whether God was with us or not. Doubt about, well, everything. And that's when that first wave came crashing in.

Sell everything and follow me, I heard in my mind. Seconds later, the second wave came crashing in: the story of the rich young ruler recorded in Mark 10 came to mind. It's all I could think about. The bridge I was crossing that day when the second wave came crashing in has now become symbolic. It took me seven years to realize the symbolism of that bridge, but God was asking me to cross from one side to the other and allow him to become the bridge that ushered me into something new. He was asking me to enter into a way of life that ditched *my* dreams and chased after *his* dreams. A way of life where I fully died to my own agenda. A way of life that *fully* trusted him. Up to that point my life was all about my dreams. It was all about how I would make my dreams come true. People ask me, "Why didn't you trust your gut when it came to buying that house?" Because I still didn't know how to trust God. I had more faith in my own judgment and abilities than I did in God. I believed I had a better future planned for us than God did. That's why. "Even after all you had been through with the kick, your decision to end your chances of kicking professionally, and your ultimate decision to get into the restaurant business? Even though you knew the cursor was flashing and that God was waiting?" Yes, even after all that, I still didn't recognize God's voice or understand the plan he had written for my life. I still didn't understand what he was doing.

As I said in the last chapter, God has a well-documented, well-orchestrated, masterful set of plans written for your life. Once you fully understand that, you will be able to weather the ups, the downs, the kicks that go wide left, and keep your eyes locked on him. I wrote that statement with what I know now. I didn't fully understand that back then. Sure, I recognized God in my life. I was one of those guys that gave him a nod of approval. Treated him like a magic genie. Thought he was here to serve my dreams and desires and not the other way around. If you get one theme out of my story, I hope it is this: *Life is not about you.* Whether you're a believer or haven't come to faith yet, I need you to know you are here for one purpose and one purpose only: to advance God's kingdom. Before you put the book down and chalk me up as "one of the crazy ones," I challenge you to stay the course and see what kind of story only God can orchestrate. It's when I chose to die to my dreams, my agenda, that God got the full permission to work on his dream and his purpose for my life. My dreams were nothing, truly nothing compared to what his dreams were for my life. But the crazy thing is the dreams that I had still managed to fit into God's dream for my life. He desires the exact same thing for you.

I immediately called Brandi and told her what had just happened. "I think I just heard God for the first time," I said. "I was driving Graham to school and out of nowhere I heard, 'Sell everything and follow me.' I'm pretty sure God wants us to sell the house and just start over. We can pay off all our personal debt and move closer to the stores. We can rent a house in Round Rock and start over." One thing you can bank on when it came to Brandi and me, we were both ready for something to happen. We were both defeated. We needed a win. If you've ever been a part of a struggling business where no matter how hard you work, it doesn't matter, you know how deflating it is. It's demoralizing. It eats you up. Not only was I letting myself down, but I felt as though I was letting my father-in-law and everyone back in Lubbock down. We found ourselves house poor. We weren't tithing. Our hope was fading—and fading fast. After a couple days of talking through it and praying about whether it was God that I heard, I called the realtor. "Hey man, Brandi and I want to put the house on the market and move over to Round Rock," I told him. "We think this will be a good move and put us a little closer to the restaurants. After thinking through everything, and looking at the big picture, this is what I think we want to ask." I still remember standing between the living room and kitchen as I gave Josh our asking price.

"I don't think you can get that, Keith. That's the top of the market in your price point, and I just don't know if we can get that."

"Remember," I said, "it's what they were asking for the house eighteen months ago. I'd love for you to come check it out in person. We repainted the entire house when we moved in. Brandi is amazing at design and staging, and I turned the extra room into a theater room. I did all the work myself, but it's pretty amazing in there."

Josh was a go-getter, and he did an awesome job of fighting for us on the purchase of that home. He represented us well, and I was hoping he'd do the same thing eighteen months later—just the other way around. A couple of days passed after of our phone conversation, and I found myself standing in the kitchen once again, discussing a strategy to sell the home with Josh. "I've got nothing negative to say about the house," he said. "Y'all have done an amazing job, and this is one of the first houses I've been in that I don't have something that needs to be put away. It's staged perfectly. But I want y'all to know, I can't guarantee anything. We can ask what you want, but I can't guarantee any showings or that you will sell at this price."

"I understand completely, but let's give it a shot."

Pictures of the house, check. Listing details, check. House clean and smellin' good, check. On March 21, 2013, I got an email from Josh: "We're live." Our home was officially on the market. Now, we wait and see. Again, we weren't sure what to expect, but God knew what to expect since he was in the driver's seat.

Showing.

Showing.

Showing.

It was showing after showing on that house. I couldn't believe it. I knew it was a great house, but I didn't expect to have that many people interested in the house on the first day especially with the price being at the top of the market. Now I've got to be truthful here. I was that creeper that when someone came to see the house, I left and pulled around the corner and watched in eager anticipation, hoping, praying.

Later that afternoon the phone rang. It was Josh. "Hey, man! I think we've got an offer coming in. I'll call you later today after I have all the details." Ahh, yes, sir! God was showing off and showing up in a big way. Day one? Really? We figured we faced an uphill battle because of our price, but to all of our surprise, we received an offer on the first day. Some might dismiss God's hand in it and say it sold so quickly because it was a great house in a great location. But no one, and I mean no one, could have ever orchestrated the next series of events. About an hour later I got another phone call from Josh. "Hey, Keith! I just got off the phone with the buyer, and they are bringing an offer. You aren't going to believe this, but not only do they want to buy the house, they want to buy *everything* in it!" God's words echoed back and forth in my mind: "Sell everything and follow me." I chuckled to myself. Not only did we sell our house, but it all happened on the first day, to the first people to look at the house, and not only did they want to buy the house, but they wanted to buy everything in it. God was showing off, and he was showing off in a way that only he could. There was more though. Not only did he perform and provide what I considered a miracle, but there were some things he needed me to learn that day. It was as though he was telling me: "I'm going to prove to you that you heard my voice and that I am who I say I am. When you listen for my voice and step out in obedience, I will show up. Are you who you say you are? You've said, 'All this stuff is temporary and doesn't go with us.' Are you willing to stand behind what you preach, or are you full of hot air and empty words? What do you say, big boy? Are you willing, truly willing to trust me and follow me?"

The challenge was on. God wanted to see what I was really made of. He was showing me that he is who he said he is, but the bigger question, the wild card in the situation, was me. He wanted to know if I was who I said I was. Was I truly willing to stand behind what I said regarding worldly things, or was I just a big talker with no real game? The invitation was on the table before me, so I did what I had to do. No empty words. No hot air. I priced it all out—furniture, art on the wall, speakers, projector, screen, the most comfortable couch I had ever sat on, the backyard furniture—everything. "Take it all! I don't care! God's got something new, and I'm ready to find out what it is." I didn't want to be the rich young ruler and go away sad. I didn't want to miss the opportunity. I didn't want to miss out on some incredible, Spirit-led, wild goose chase of an adventure because I wrapped my worth up in worldly things. You see, Jesus gives us a glimpse of what he missed out on when he told the disciples, "no one who has left home or brothers or sisters or mother or father or children or fields for me and the gospel will fail to receive a hundred times as much in this present age: homes, brothers, sisters, mothers, children and fields—along with persecutions—and in the age to come eternal life. But many who are first will be last, and the last first" (Mark 10:29–31). I was tired of putting myself first. I had what so many wanted. I had the accolades, the trophies and awards, and experience playing Division 1 college football. I had the well-paying job and great house. I had the American dream, but all of it was meaningless—every bit of it. I was ready to be last. What exactly did that mean? I wasn't 100 percent sure, but I wanted to find out. I wanted to know—no, check that—I *had* to know what the rich young ruler walked away from.

"Sell everything and follow me."

MEDITATIONS WITH ROSWELL

A wise man once told me, "God's kingdom life is made available to everyone, and everyone can afford it. But it will cost you everything." I humbly pray that it doesn't take tragedy, loss, or some massive failure for us as people to see what God truly has for each and every one of us; but I dare to ask: What type of person are you? What would it take for you to "sell everything" and follow a plan where many of the details (if not all of the details) are foreign and completely unknown to you?

7

THE MARCH

As we sat across from one another in that local coffee shop at the end of 2019, Jon listened intently as I told him the story. After a few minutes of taking it in, he looked me directly in the eye and with confidence said, "You're the rich young ruler. You're just some modern-day version of him. Look, you upheld all the rules. You've never been drunk. You and your wife saved yourselves for marriage. You honored your parents. You name it, you did it—exactly how the rich young ruler lived his life. But unlike him, you did what he couldn't do. You sold it all, and look at the story that God has produced in your life." That was literally the first time I'd ever made that connection. It blew my mind. Was he right? Could I be living out what the rich young ruler missed out on? Listen, God won't, and doesn't, reveal everything directly to you. Sometimes God brings insight and revelation through our brothers or sisters in Christ. Sometimes he moves in ways we personally can't see, but he reveals his truth to others about us, so they can speak his truth, his revelation, into our lives. God's ways are not our ways. "As the heavens are higher than the earth, so are my ways higher than your ways and my thoughts than your thoughts" (Isaiah 55:9). We can't fully understand the ways that he moves or how he operates. His ways are mysterious, and like any good mystery, he wants you and me to search for him with everything in our being to seek him out as if you are searching and digging for that next great business deal that'll produce millions, because once you find him, all bets are off. Once you find him, you step into the greatest adventure your mind can't even begin to fathom.

THE BEGINNING OF THE END

I did a Jericho march multiple times around the two restaurants with one of my best friends, a man of God, Marty Baker. You might be thinking, *What's a Jericho March?* In Joshua 6, God gives Joshua, the leader of Israel, a directive to overtake the city of Jericho by having the army of Israel, and all of the priests, march around the walls of the city, one time per day, for six days. On the seventh day, they were to march around the city seven times as the priests blew their trumpets. On the seventh trip around, when the priests sounded a long blast on their trumpets, then all of Israel was to give a shout. When they did, the walls of Jericho would come down and the people of God were to overtake the city. As Marty and I marched around those stores, we prayed that God would use them to advance his kingdom. We prayed that God would use those restaurants for his glory—to fund and expand the work and workers of the greatest kingdom known to man. We prayed and prayed, and we prayed some more, but the restaurants didn't make it. We had to shut the doors for good. There I was confused again—the understatement of the year. I prayed: *I did what you asked me to do. I sold it all. Why, God, why? I feel like we've been through this multiple times now. I follow your prompting, experience a spiritual high, the peak, only to feel the terrifying plummet into the valley, a spiritual low.*

As the heavens are higher than the earth, so are my ways higher than your ways and my thoughts than your thoughts.

I really wanted those restaurants to thrive. In my natural mind I thought that if those restaurants were successful financially, then God could use them to advance his kingdom. The reality was my natural mind became a black hole of uncertainty, doubt, and fear.

God was never after my natural mind. In fact, from the moment you and I were born, he has been after one thing: your kingdom mind, my kingdom mind, and the kingdom mind of every person who walks the face of the earth. From Adam to the last person who will ever walk the streets of this earth one day, he wants our kingdom mind as he desires to develop a kingdom strategy within us.

The enemy unfortunately stole this in the garden of Eden, but God's antidote was sending his Son, Jesus, to re-establish his kingdom here on earth. Not everyone will grasp this call or accept this call. But when we do, we just have to be willing to pick up our cross and follow him and remember that just as the heavens are higher than the earth, so are his ways higher than our ways and his thoughts than our thoughts (See Matthew 16:24 and Isaiah 55:9).

At the time I had no clue that this would be the beginning of the end for me in the restaurant business. I had no clue that God had a completely different story written for my life. You see, I was trying to force my way in life, to create what I thought would be my best life. I was on a mission to advance *my* kingdom. I was on a mission to be a successful businessman in the eyes of the world—in the eyes of my family—in the eyes of myself. I wanted what the rich young ruler wanted, to be recognized for my goodness by God, while doing what was in the best interest of me, myself, and I. Read that last sentence again. Does that sound like anyone you know? Does it sound like you?

The problem was I had inserted myself smack-dab in the middle of religion, and I just… couldn't… see it. The story of the rich young ruler was eye opening for me. He represents so many of us, so many. If we're truly honest about our society and our culture, it's scary. It's scary to see how many of us miss out on the adventure of a lifetime all because we are consumed—no, obsessed—with the little *k* king. On the flip side, it can be scary good. Scary good, because if we could realize who we are in the kingdom and grasp onto our wiring and his kingdom identity for us, then watch out world—watch out!

God may not call you to sell it all like he did with me. He may do something completely different with your life, but here is what I've learned about God when it comes to me and when it comes to you: he wants all of you. He wants you to fully trust him. He wants you to stop finding your worth in your works, your deeds, your money, your status, your goodness, your business savvy, your you name it. He's ready for you to chase after him and sell out for his kingdom. For me, I needed to sell it all. I needed to stop finding my worth in what people thought of me. For you, the story may look, and feel, totally different, but here is one thing you can take to the bank, and it ain't money. God wants to develop a kingdom strategy within you. He wants you to understand your identity and how he wired you, because once you begin to understand your identity and how he wired you, then you can become the mighty warrior he created you to be. He's ready. He's ready for you to step into your calling as a kingdom warrior, sword drawn, standing your ground confidently because the God of the universe, the Creator of it all walked you into his armor room and outfitted you with his kingdom armor. I can envision it now. Unsure of yourself you step into the room, not knowing if you really are the person for the job. You speak up, "Me? Are you sure you have the right person? I'm not so sure I'm qualified." He pays no attention to the doubtful and demeaning words spoken by his warrior. Instead, he wraps the belt of truth around your waist. Immediately he grabs the breastplate of righteousness and rests it upon your shoulders. He covers your feet with the gospel of peace, and he hands you the shield of faith that is impenetrable against the attacks of the evil one. He steps back, admires his handiwork as he takes a quick scan, grabs the helmet of salvation, and fits it securely to your head. He steps back again, and studies you for a moment more intently. He looks you over just as a tailor would after outfitting you with that custom made suit. Up. Down. Left. Right. He asks you to turn and face the other direction. *Perfect. It is good*, he thinks to himself. He's satisfied. As he admires his handiwork, he realizes there is one thing missing. He steps around the corner and grabs his weapon of choice: the sword of his Spirit. He approaches you confidently as he places it in your hands knowing that his Word, the sword of his Spirit, will undoubtedly prevail as you step out as the mighty warrior for his kingdom that you were always destined to be.

HERE WE GO AGAIN...

I was completely broken, depressed. I felt like a complete and utter failure. I wasn't moving forward in my career. In fact, I was moving backward. I wasn't treading water. I was drowning, failing. And as an achiever, that's about the worst emotion one can feel—worthless, without purpose. There I was, broken and full of doubt about why I was on this earth, but once again it was in my brokenness that God began his work of developing a kingdom strategy within me. I began to feel as though after seven years that the restaurant business may not be what I was called to do. I was thirty years old with two young kids and one on the way. I had a family that needed me, but once again, I was at a loss about what to do.

For much of my life I had felt a call to write but had never pursued it. All of a sudden that feeling came rushing back in. After years of feedback from teachers and those close to me, it seemed clear that God had given me a talent for writing and a unique perspective on life. Was now the time? I found myself in exploration mode, so during my thirtieth year, I began to write a book, and I've got to tell you, it was a powerful concept. I put in the work each morning at five o'clock before I went to work. I did the research, wrote the sample chapters, put together the book proposal, only to get denied. And denied. And denied. Over and over again the same answer kept coming back. No. I didn't have the credentials in the world's eyes. I was a mid-level manager at a local taco shop. That was it. I hadn't gone to seminary. I wasn't a pastor. I didn't have a doctorate. I didn't work in the field of psychology. I didn't even own any businesses. Basically, what I was being told is, "You don't have the authority nor the credentials to write on the subject." The subject God had given me, mind you, but I didn't hold those keys. The answer kept coming back as a heartbreaking no. Maybe the time wasn't right, and maybe God was just planting the seed, but in the meantime, here came that question once again, "What do you want to do?"

Seven years had passed from the first time Brandi asked me that question, but here it was sitting on a plate in front of me once again. Just like before, I had no clue what I wanted to do with my life, but that was the question that loomed over me as the leader of our family. "I don't know. I just don't know what I'm good at." You see, I struggled massively with my identity. I was still cloaked by the devil. I thought I knew who I was. I thought I was called to write, but I guess the world didn't think so, or maybe the time wasn't right. So now what?

Brandi came with another question, but this time it was more specific, more pointed. "What about homebuilding?" she asked. There's a wild, audacious, off the wall thought, but it really intrigued me. Deep down, I have more of an artistic mind. I like to envision something, work through the process of completing the masterpiece, and then start fresh with a new idea, a new concept. I liked that idea, but I had no clue where to start.

During our first seven years of marriage, Brandi and I lived in seven different places. Seven places to call home and seven places for Brandi to practice her God-given gift of design. She has a degree in sociology, not design, but unlike me, no one could deny her from exercising her God-given talent. Brandi has been gifted in design since she was a little girl, but it really revealed itself at our first apartment after we were married. The property manager stopped by to check on us after moving in, took one look inside, and asked if we'd be willing to have our place be the show apartment for a discount on our monthly rent. Um, yes, please! Anything helps as newlyweds. She was still in school, and I was just starting my career, so every single dollar mattered.

As we moved around to those seven different places, every single one of them was more than a place to call home or rest our head; it was Brandi's canvas—a masterpiece ready to be stroked by its creator. Each place was a studio for her to hone her talent. And that's exactly what she did. We became accidental flippers. We didn't purposely look at a home and think, "Oh, that's a great house we can make a lot of money on." Nope. We thought, "This looks like a great place to call home and raise our family." Never in a million years did we intend to flip homes, but that's what happened when the restaurant business needed us somewhere else. That was when I was building my kingdom, so I was willing to do anything I could to get to the top, to make the money, to get what I wanted—all while I "lived for the Lord."

We are all guilty at some point of a man-centered kingdom, but even when believers attempt to rule their lives, the God of the universe is right by our side patiently waiting for us to come to a different realization; he's ready for us to have a paradigm shift. It's as if God was saying, "Your kingdom may stand for a while. It's possible it may thrive for a time, but inevitably, it will fall. My kingdom, though, my kingdom will never fall. My kingdom has stood, and will continue to stand, forever! I am the Alpha and the Omega, who was, and who is, and who is yet to come, the Almighty. So why don't you come on over, build in my kingdom, and let me set you free?"

So that's what we did. I gave it all up, opened my hands, and said, "Lord, if this is what you desire out of my life, then as I turn the handle of the door that's in front of me, let it open. Your will be done, not mine." My attempts at building a kingdom had failed, but God was inviting me to something new—something fresh—something heavenly.

"As the heavens are higher than the earth, so are my ways higher than your ways and my thoughts than your thoughts" (Isaiah 55:9).

MEDITATIONS WITH ROSWELL

Have you ever experienced what many call a spiritual high only to find yourself completely wrecked, broken, and depressed in the valley? A place where you begin to ask God, "Why?" Have you ever found yourself questioning your purpose or why you are even on this earth? You may wonder, *if God is shutting every door I come upon, even after complete surrender and obedience, how can there possibly be a plan for my life?* Find your peace, your rest, and your hope in Isaiah 55:9.

8

THE SELF-MADE MAN

As I dialed the number, I had no clue what to expect. What would he say? How would he react to the words as they left my mouth? Would he be gracious to my request, or would he dismiss me as just another guy with a dream? This time, though, before I dialed that number, I took my request, my dream, my desire, and I laid it at my Father's feet. "Lord, if this is what you want for my life," I prayed, "if this is the path you want us to go down, would you make it undeniable as you open the doors to the people who will help me navigate this new adventure? Let them be positive about their experience and let it be abundantly clear that this is what you want us to do." Over three thousand days have passed since I prayed that prayer and many prayers like it, but I can remember those prayers, and the feelings of hope, like they were yesterday.

"Hey, Jordan, this is Keith Toogood. Do you have a few minutes you could spare?" I asked into the phone. The anxiety began to mount, my heart began to race, and my breathing became a little quicker as the next question got closer to my lips. I had to ask the question, or it would never happen. Here we go… "Would you be willing to teach me the home-building business?"

Without hesitation, Jordan replied, "Yeah, man, I'd love to teach you."

Wait. What? Was he serious? This guy knows me, but it's not like we are best friends or anything. And he's willing to say yes just like that?

"Are you serious? Dude! Thank you! Do I need to come work for you so I can learn the ropes?"

"No. Just build one."

Just build one. Therein lay the problem. I don't think he understood that my home building experience was literally at the bottom of the barrel. Zero. Zilch. Nada.

Just build one, I thought as I tried to take that in. *I don't have any earthly idea where to even begin, but I guess we can hammer that out later.*

Then to Jordan I continued, "Are you at all concerned that I could potentially be competition and take some of your market share?"

"Nah, man. There is enough land out here. More than enough to go around."

"You say to just build one like it's that simple, but are you positive I don't need to come work for you for a couple of years?"

"Yeah, I'm positive. If I train you up knowing that your plan is to go out on your own, it will help me for a little while. Then I'm going to have to start all over and train someone else in a couple of years. Just go build one. I'll help you on your first one. I'll get you connected with Lubbock Land Company so you can get a lot. And I'll connect you with a banker. Let's meet at six o'clock for breakfast later this week, and I'll help you get on the right path."

When I hung up the phone, I couldn't believe what had just happened. This dude who had been in the home-building business for nine years just agreed to be my mentor. No hesitation. No fear of competition. Nothing. He just wanted to help me get on a path that would create opportunity for my family and me. Instead of a scarcity mentality that wanted to keep it all to himself, he had an abundance mentality that knew there was more than enough for a portion to be shared. It was some of the best news I had heard in a long time, but there were realities on the other side of that phone call that had to be considered. Realities such as life, responsibility, family.

LAUNCHING PAD

I had a wife, two kids, and third one on the way, and they were depending on me to put a roof over their head, clothes on their back, and food on the table. It could take nine months to a year for me to realize any income on a house that we sold, and that was a massive question mark because who knew if we could even sell one. I needed another job that would allow me to check on a house before work, at lunch, and after work. Jordan had told me that he started that very same way, so I called people in my network. Blake Buchanan, who is the founder of Bahama Bucks and the "Greatest Sno on Earth," was all for it. He said, "I once had a dream like yours, and I want to do anything I can to help guys with an entrepreneurial spirit reach their goal. Give me all you've got for at least a year, and if the time is right for you and Brandi, y'all can hit the road and start pursuing your dream of building homes."

My good friend Grant Gafford, who owned a battery store called Battery Joe said, "Why don't you come do some consulting work with us for a few months before you go to work for Bahama Bucks? I'd like a fresh set of eyes on our operation, and I'd like for you to bring some of your experience from the restaurant business into Battery Joe. Let's see how we can improve the operation." Doors were flying open left and right as we began to walk down this new path God was clearing for us.

Then I got connected with Ron Reeves. Ron and I had some things in common. Ron was the quarterback for Texas Tech from 1978 to 1981 and had been building homes and commercial buildings in Lubbock for many years. He and I went to the same church but had never met. Through a conversation with my pastor, Brad, he thought to connect us as I started this new journey. Ron and I met for breakfast, and he agreed to help out in any way that he could. He spoke so positively about the business which was an answer to my prayers. He said it would have many challenges and could be difficult, but he absolutely loved the business.

Then there was Jordan. I owe Jordan a standing ovation for his willingness to mentor me. At the time, we didn't know it, but without his mentorship, this book wouldn't have made it to your hands, and you and I would quite possibly still be under the horrific cloaking of the enemy.

Jordan truly became an incredible mentor to me as I ventured into this new business. He'd meet me for breakfast once a week and pour out all he knew. He didn't just give it all away though. He expected me to work, to dig, to have to search for the information I needed. He knew that if I searched for the answers on my own, I'd retain the knowledge at a deeper level. He'd give me homework assignments to report on at the next week's breakfast. He connected me with Sharon from Lubbock Land Company so I could buy my first lot, and he poured his time and energy into me as I began to wrap my head around this new business. He answered the phone, and when I say he answered the phone, I mean he answered the phone a lot. If you know anything about me, it's that I like to ask a lot of questions, so I was constantly blowing Jordan up. And he answered every single one of the questions I threw his way. He was everything you could want in a mentor and more.

I can only imagine that this is how Timothy felt as he began to experience the leadership and mentorship of Paul. What a blessing it is to have someone walk alongside you as you learn and grow from their experiences, wisdom, and knowledge. When Paul entered the town of Lystra and learned that Timothy was a disciple whom "people spoke well of," from that point on, we see Paul mentoring and shaping Timothy into a great leader of the early church. Does Timothy become such a leader without the help of Paul? Only God knows the answer to that, but here is what I take away from their relationship. Godly mentorship becomes a launching pad that will exponentially accelerate the mentee into a different stratosphere. A mentoring relationship is a launching pad that will blast the mentee to levels they couldn't achieve on their own, a launching pad that places them smack-dab in the epicenter of the BOOM.

TIME TO OOZE

This might be the place where I step on some toes—and I have a feeling that a lot of pride is about to ooze out of some folks, but this is the place where we make a declaration. A place where we build an altar, never to be forgotten, as we humbly approach the King of kings as we ask for forgiveness. This is a place where we destroy a nearly two-century-year-old lie and then bury it never to be heard from again.

There is no such thing.

It doesn't exist.

And you. Aren't. One.

There is no such thing as a self-made man!

First, from a scientific standpoint, it's impossible. You didn't create yourself out of nothing—that would make you God. We don't need to have the birds and the bees talk here, do we? Second, of course, everyone knows we didn't create ourselves out of nothingness, but the idea that you and you alone willed yourself into the position you are in today because you *made* yourself is absurd. The term *self-made man* means that you have had zero influence from any outside source. Zero. That you somehow managed to learn everything, and I mean every single thing that you know, completely on your own, is insane.

The term *self-made man* was coined by a United States Senator on February 2, 1842, when he described individuals whose success lay within the individuals themselves, not with outside conditions. With all due respect, sir, you were wrong then, and you're wrong today. You fed a lie that people have believed for nearly two centuries, and it's time to stop that lie dead in its tracks.

Self-made man...no sir! You are the product and result of a God who formed you in your mother's womb—a God who knows you inside and out—a God who knows the hairs on your head—a God who knows everything, and I mean everything about you. He knit you so perfectly, so intricately, so purposefully, and just like the potter with clay, he has been shaping you and molding you from the moment your heart beat for the first time inside your mother's womb.

You are the product of countless family members, teachers, coaches, or friends. You are the product of generations of people who would pass down an inheritance with the hopes that the next generation would learn from them and then improve upon what they were able to accomplish. You didn't create the sounds that each letter makes to then teach yourself how to read and write. You didn't formulate the mathematics that helps you succeed today. You didn't create every single tool and resource that you use on a daily basis. Nope. You are no self-made man. You are a God-made man put on this earth to do exactly what he has called you to do. Period. End of discussion.

You might be thinking to yourself, "Keith, calm down, you're taking the phrase 'self-made man' too far." Am I? With all due respect, the apostle Paul tells us, "A little yeast works through the whole batch of dough" (Galatians 5:9). One little lie can destroy it all. One simple, little lie can have people believing that they are a little *g* god who is able to create whatever they desire, that it's some kind of secret. Man, I hate that book, *The Secret*. Self-made men have led us to believe that through the power of positive thinking we can do anything and everything we put our mind to. It's literally the oldest trick in the book. See the garden of Eden. We have been trying to steal God's identity since the garden of Eden. Remember that? Satan had convinced Adam and Eve in Genesis 3 that they would be like God if they just ate from the tree of the knowledge of good and evil—that they could do what he could do—that they could be like him. That he, Adam, could become a self-made man. But wait, there's more. "When the woman saw that the fruit of the tree was good for food and pleasing to the eye, and also desirable for gaining wisdom, she took some and ate it. She also gave some to her husband, who was with her, and he ate it" (Genesis 3:6). Before we go any further, we've got to stop blaming Eve. Adam wasn't off in some other part of the garden tending the land and taking care of some other trees or animals. He was there! He was right there next to Eve listening to the whole conversation. He had every opportunity to end the conversation, but he didn't. He didn't step up to the plate. He didn't man up and protect Eve. He didn't stand on what he knew to be right. He folded. He, like Eve, so desperately wanted what the devil was selling. **He wanted to be like God**. You have to see this! That was the temptation that the devil threw out. Stop and think about this for a moment. The fruit was from the tree of the knowledge of good and evil. Adam and Eve didn't know evil. Up to that point they hadn't experienced evil, so how could they even comprehend that temptation? Here is what they could comprehend: "You can be like God."

Everything that God had done up to that point was in his words good. So the temptation wasn't necessarily just the knowledge of good and evil, it was that they could be like God. That they could create like him—that they could breathe life into whatever they desired. That they could possess the same power that God possessed—that they could make themselves into whatever they desired to be—that they could be self-made—that they could be wise like God and make it all happen on their own. It was a lie. All lies!

Don't eat the fruit! Instead, humbly prostrate yourself at the foot of the throne of the King of kings and thank him for his goodness and mercy. Thank him for every single person that he has placed on your path whether they are family, friend, coach, or mentor because every single one of them has been a gift from God that has helped shape the person that you are today. Be like Timothy. Learn and grow as you study from the godly men who go before you. Be like Paul. Raise up a generation and mentor those around you as you advance the kingdom of God. Be like Jordan. Pour into a friend so they can become everything that God created them to be.

THE LIST

I'm going to end this chapter with a list of people that I would consider mentors and/or people who challenged me to become the best version of who God created me to be. For me, this was a powerful exercise as I reflect back on the entirety of my life. As you read this list, my prayer is that it brings people from your life to the forefront of your mind. When you finish this chapter, I'd encourage you to make a list as well. Grab a notebook, your phone, or grab a seat at your computer and reflect on all of the people God has placed in your life—the people he has placed on your path that have helped shape you into the person you are today. For me, each one of the people below has had a major impact in my development whether they knew it or not, and I thank God for placing them in my life. I am no self-made man. I am the product and result of the God who formed me in my mother's womb—the God who knows me inside and out—the God who knows the hairs on my head—the God who knows everything, and I mean everything about me. He knit me so perfectly, so intricately, so purposefully, and just like the potter with clay, he has been shaping me and molding me from the moment my heart beat for the first time inside my mother's womb. There are countless people who have been on this journey, and I'm sure I'm going to forget many on this list, so please forgive me, but if you were a teacher, coach, friend, or mentor, thank you for the impact you have had in my life. Thank you for challenging me to become everything that God intended me to be. And thank you for never giving up on me.

Dad (R.I.P. I'll see you again someday!)
Mom
Brian
Gayland and Brenda Avance (R.I.P), Brandon and Tim
Richard and Yvonne Cox
Adam Harden
Marty Baker
Coach Mike Wheeler

Coach Tony Felker
Mrs. Seabourn
Mrs. Witcher
Mrs. Brooks (R.I.P.)
Bennie Wylie
Ruffin McNeil
Dennis Simmons
Jon Randles (R.I.P.)
John Strappazon
Rocky Willingham
Mark Reese
Greg Blankenship
Freddy Olivarez
Art Parrish
Mike Mendoza
Grant Gafford
Blake Buchanan
Jordan Wheatley
Ron Reeves
Mike Foster
Rick Betenbough (R.I.P.)
Brad Ingram, Tommy Politz, and Jonathan Mast—
the teaching team at Hillside Christian Church
Roswell Smith Jr.
Steve Hoggard
Scott Montgomery
Andy Bean
Derrick Merchant
Jeffrey Taylor (R.I.P.)
J. Long
Wes Yoder
Kobus Grobler
Boniface "B.B." Shonga

Brandon Fannin

Todd Truesdell

And saving the best for last, my beautiful bride, Brandi Toogood. You've taught me more than you know and have challenged me to be the best version of myself. You are a gift from God, and I wouldn't be here without your love and support!

MEDITATIONS WITH ROSWELL

This chapter underscores and digs right at the heart of every man's fall: PRIDE. No man is an island, and no man is self-made. I challenge you to invest some time and build a robust list of the people that have contributed to "making" you.

9

THE VOICE

Many years have passed since I met Jordan at Tech Café for that first breakfast, and I'd be lying if I didn't tell you that uncertainty, doubt, frustration, questions, anxiety, and even depression still rear their ugly head on occasion. But when they do, I have learned to anchor myself in what David said in Psalm 23: "Even though I walk through the valley of the shadow of death, I will fear no evil, for you are with me; your rod and your staff they comfort me" (Psalm 23:4 ESV). As fear and doubt made their attempt to occupy my mind, God has taught me to find strength through my shepherd, Christ, and it has brought hope, joy, contentment, and a complete trust in God Almighty. Needless to say, that first decade of homebuilding was crazy—a wild goose chase. Yet through it all, these truths equally remind me that God never left me nor forsook me (Hebrews 13:5). His words sustained me. They were a lamp unto my feet and a light unto my path (Psalm 119:105). I was confident that God, who began a good work in me, would carry it on to completion (Philippians 1:6). There were times when I had much, and there were times when I had little. But I learned the secret of being content in any and every situation, whether well fed or hungry, whether living in plenty or want. I found that I could do all things through Christ who gave me strength (Philippians 4:12–13).

Before we go any further, can we address the reference to the last verse? In my opinion, this is one of the most misused verses out of God's Holy Word. We cherry pick verse 13 and plaster it on mugs, shirts, and bumper stickers, and athletes use it as a way to generate success for the field or the court they are about to step upon—that because they operate out of Christ's strength, it's going to give them the ability to make super-natural plays that will win the game for their team. I've got news for you. Verse 13 is not about your prosperity. Verse 13 is not about some super-human strength that's going to allow you to succeed because you call on the name of Jesus Christ. He's no magic genie. No, verse 13 is all about sustaining ourselves in the hope we find in Christ—that no matter if we miss wide left, fall flat on our face, or experience incredible success, we can be content whatever the circumstance. Why? Because we find our strength is sustained through Jesus Christ our Lord (See Philippians 4:11–12). Verse 13 is the antidote to verses 11 and 12. To live is Christ and to die is gain (Philippians 1:21). And because I know that verse to be absolute truth, I can do all things through Christ who gives me strength.

THE PEOPLE

After two years of working at Battery Joe with my good friend Grant, it was time for Brandi and me to launch out on our own. That decision was both exhilarating and terrifying all at the same time. We had built a few houses that could sustain our family, but we definitely weren't in the clear. Money was stretched thin, and we had a six-year-old, a four-year-old, and a two-year-old depending on us to put food on the table. We were able to meet the necessities of life, but beyond that, there weren't many dollars left over at the end of each month.

"You need to hire Scott." The words came out of nowhere one day. Completely out of left field, but I knew it was the voice of the Lord. There was no doubt in my mind who it was, as the only person named Scott I knew at the time was my first cousin Scott Montgomery. Scott and I had both grown up in the Dallas area and both resided in Lubbock, but we didn't see each other often. We were both busy trying to make ends meet for our families. When we did see each other, it was the typical family get-together: Christmas, Easter, or the occasional summer cookout that also included some family pictures. I think it was around 1996 when our extended family got together and took those family pics: red and blue braces, some tube socks, and the haircut of a life-time—an epic, butt cut, undercut chili bowl. I was rockin' it. Nevertheless, I couldn't shake what the Lord had said: "You need to hire Scott." I filed that away in the corner of my brain and placed it in the folder called When God Speaks. We were barely making it as it was. I knew there was no way we could afford to hire an employee, so maybe that was God just planting a seed that would grow sometime out in the future.

God had other plans.

The next day my phone rang. I pulled it out of my pocket, looked at the screen, and slid the button to the right to answer the call. "Hey, man, what's up?" My very normal day was about to get flipped upside down because the words God had spoken just the day before began to race through my mind as I saw the name Scott Montgomery appear on that screen. I remember this conversation like it was yesterday, and word for word, this is how it went down.

"Hey, man, not much," Scott responded. "I know you're a busy guy, so I won't take much of your time, but I've been thinking. If you ever need to hire someone, I'd love to come work for you."

Say what? You can't make this stuff up! In less than twenty-four hours God set his plan into motion. I didn't know it. Scott didn't know it. Brandi didn't know it. In fact, no one knew it except for one. God knew. And when God plans it, buckle up because he's about to take you on the adventure of a lifetime. To be completely transparent I didn't immediately tell Scott, "You're hired! Start tomorrow!" No. I delayed. I didn't have the faith I do now, and as I said, Brandi and I were barely making it as it was. We could barely pay ourselves, let alone add another salary to the equation, so I told Scott, "Let me think on it and pray on it." I delayed. I had doubts—I had questions—I had fears—and all of those took ahold of me and gripped me tightly as I wrestled with what God had told me to do.

IN THEIR SHOES

I said it in the intro to this book, and I'll say it again: I'm no different than you. What's more, as I study the characters in the holy pages of Scripture, we are really no different than them either. We are all fully human and fully broken. Doubts, fears, and questions ran through their minds as they wrestled with what God had asked them to do, but if we will do what they did and fully trust God, then we can also do what they did and impact a generation for his kingdom. Like Moses we can convince a king to bow to the authority of God Almighty even though we have a stuttering problem. You say you come from nothing, that your family is a bunch of nobodies, and that you're the least of all the nobodies in your family? Great! God can position you to turn an entire nation away from idol worship as you lead people back to the King of kings just as Gideon did. Maybe you can save an entire city like Jonah did even though he ran in the complete opposite direction when God originally called him. How about Peter who declared Jesus was the son of God in Matthew 16:16 but later allowed fear to creep in as he denied knowing Jesus three times in Matthew 26? Thankfully, though, God's grace flowed through his Son, and Peter, by the power of the Holy Spirit, went on to set the first century church on fire. Who's to say we can't do the same kind of things as we allow the Holy Spirit to be our advocate and counselor?

Jesus never promised that following him would be easy. In fact, he told his disciples just the opposite. There will be troubles. There will be persecution. There will be doubt, fear, anxiety, questions, and so much more, but the reward. Oh, how sweet the reward will be. Those twelve men that were sitting around Jesus didn't have what we have today. They didn't have the Bible to study. They didn't have a Strong's concordance. They were getting all the teaching in real time, so they definitely didn't get the opportunity to study history as they took it all in. They are the history!

They had questions. They didn't understand. They compared themselves to one another—to the rich young ruler—to everything that was going on around them. They were doing their best to understand what in the world was going on as they followed this guy named Jesus. Then as Jesus sits down to have one final meal with these twelve men, he lays it all out to them. He tells them that he is going to go away, that he is going to die for the sins of the world and that he will no longer be with them. Now I want you to put yourself in their shoes for just a moment and imagine that you are one of those twelve men. You listen as your Master, the Son of God, tells you that he has to go away and that he is going to die. Imagine the heartbreak. Maybe even feelings of abandonment begin to set in. Questions begin to race through your mind. You might even speak up and say, "No, Lord, stay with us. My life has been incredible since I found you. I enjoy our talks. I enjoy your teaching. To watch people fall to their knees as they humbly acknowledge the greatness of who you are is mind piercing. You can't go away. Life is too good with you here. I need you here with me."

God had other plans.

Plans that were greater than any of them could comprehend. Plans that laid out another promise that was yet to come. What is that promise you might ask? The Holy Spirit—the Advocate—the Counselor. As Jesus and the disciples have one final meal together, Jesus begins to lay out the role of the Holy Spirit as he simultaneously makes them a promise: "But very truly I tell you, it is for your good that I am going away. Unless I go away, the Advocate will not come to you; but if I go, I will send him to you. . . . But when he, the Spirit of truth, comes, he will guide you into all the truth. He will not speak on his own, but will speak only what he hears, and he will tell you what is yet to come. He will glorify me because it is from me that he will receive what he will make known to you. All that belongs to the Father is mine. That is why I said the Spirit will receive from me what he will make known to you. . . . I have told you these things, so that in me you may have peace. In this world you will have trouble. But take heart! I have overcome the world" (John 16:7, 13–14, 33).

Remember that little verse we found in Philippians 4:13, the one that talks about being able to do all things through Christ that we plaster on T-shirts, bumper stickers, and mugs? This is what it means. Take heart! I can do all things through Christ who gives me strength. This life is not my own. I was bought with a price, and so were you. To hear God say, "Well done!" is worth it all to me. I'll sell everything and follow you, Lord! We'll follow you on an adventure that will take our breath way. We'll follow you on an adventure that will leave us rich with relationship. We'll follow you on an adventure that leaves us asking, "What's next?"

Follow Him.

Follow Him.

Follow Him.

As it is written in John 14:6: "I am the way and the truth and the life. No one comes to the Father except through me." If you are a follower of Christ, I'm willing to bet that you've heard that scripture before, but as I studied that verse while writing this, the next verse jumped off the page. It's like it was screaming, "Look at me. Look at me!" We don't quote verse 7, but it seals the deal and fires me up all the more. Verse 7 says this: "If you really know me, you will know my Father as well. From now on, you do know him and have seen him." Let's take a moment and look at what Jesus didn't say. Jesus didn't say, "If you know me." He didn't say, "If you kind of know me." He didn't say, "If you acknowledge that you know me." No, he draws a line in the sand, quantifies it, then drives a stake into the ground, and says, "If you *really* know me, then you will know my father as well" (John 14:7, emphasis mine). This life isn't just about believing in him. It's about really knowing him.

Recently, God wrecked me of "believing in him" when I asked my boy J. Long if a guy he was in talks with was a believer. God quickly corrected me and had me ask a different question. The question God wanted me to ask was this: "Is he a follower? Is he a follower of Christ?" When I shared this same question and conviction with my buddy Todd, a light bulb went off in Todd's head. He said, "Jesus never told the disciples, 'Drop your nets and believe in me.' No, he said, 'Drop your nets and follow me.' " It's never been just about believing in him. It's about chasing him with everything you've got so you can really know him, and when you really know him, then you know the Father as well (John 10:30, 14:11). What a promise!

THE REST OF THE STORY

Did you ever get the opportunity to listen to Paul Harvey growing up? Every morning and afternoon on the way to and from school we'd listen to Paul Harvey. Without a doubt my favorite segment was always *The Rest of the Story*. He'd tie up loose ends. He'd get into the details of incredible stories and break them down further as he revealed some unknown facts buried deep inside the story. But my favorite thing of all was that the man could flat-out tell a story. He truly was a masterful storyteller. So in my best Paul Harvey voice, we're going to dig a little deeper as we dive into the rest of the story.

As I said before, these guys didn't want Jesus to leave them. This guy named Jesus had changed their life! They had the opportunity to go on the adventure of a lifetime with Jesus Christ, the Son of God. They talked to him. They listened to him. They grew exponentially in their faith because they were in his presence. They were, without a doubt, living their best life, but they didn't know what they didn't know. You see, Jesus is the God-man—fully God and fully human. So being fully human, he did human things. He'd go off on his own and spend time with his Father in prayer. He'd eat, drink, and sleep. In fact, in one famous scripture found in Luke 8, Jesus was asleep on a boat as a raging storm tossed it about. His disciples finally woke him up as a last-ditch effort to save themselves as they feared for their lives. Jesus stood up, rebuked the wind and waters, and the storm subsided. In an instant, all was calm. Then in the most epic mic drop moment ever, Jesus turned to his disciples and asked, "Where is your faith?" (Luke 8:25). In other words, he asked, "Do you not know who I am?" What these guys didn't understand when Jesus says, "It's better for you that I go away" (John 16:7 NLT), is that the promise of the Holy Spirit was just on the other side.

Although Jesus is fully human, he knew no sin. So being fully human, he couldn't communicate with each of them simultaneously. He couldn't be in their presence one hundred percent of the time. When he went off on his own to pray, the disciples were also left on their own. When he was asleep in that boat, it literally meant he was asleep, which means he wasn't speaking to them. But the promise that Jesus gives in John 14–16 was near. It was so close these twelve men could nearly taste it. Jesus himself promised that what they were about to experience would be better. The time was coming when Jesus would carry his cross, die for the sins of the world, and return to his Father in heaven, but in a beautiful turn of events, the presence of God that rested upon Jesus as found in Isaiah 11:2, while he walked the earth, would rest on and inhabit everyone who really knew him.

Pay attention to this, please pay attention to this. Jesus told his disciples when they were having one last meal and celebrating the Passover in the upper room: "Don't you believe that I am in the Father, and that the Father is in me? The words I say to you I do not speak on my own authority. Rather, it is the Father living in me, who is doing his work" (John 14:10). Jesus reinforced this truth once more when he told his disciples: "These words you hear are not my own; they belong to the Father who sent me" (John 14:24). As he wrapped it all up, Jesus confirmed his deity one more time: "But when he, the Spirit of Truth comes, he will guide you into all the truth. He will not speak on his own; he will speak only what he hears, and he will tell you what is yet to come. He will glorify me because it is from me that he will receive what he will make known to you. All that belongs to the Father is mine. That is why I said the Spirit will receive from me what he will make known to you" (John 16:13–15).

So why was it better for Jesus to go away? Because the same Spirit that filled him while he walked this earth as a human would inhabit and speak to all who really know him. Why? Because the blood of Christ covered our sin, finally redeeming the human race, and allowing our body to become the dwelling place for the Father, Son, and Holy Spirit. The veil has been torn! Jesus didn't speak on his own. He spoke what belonged to the Father. The Holy Spirit doesn't speak on his own. He only speaks what he hears from the Father through Jesus. Do you see the beauty of this? Jesus said, it is better for you that I go away, because what you hear me speak comes not from me but from the Father. When he was off praying on his own, they couldn't hear the Father. When Jesus was alone with Peter, James, and John, the other nine couldn't hear the Father. When he was asleep in that boat, they couldn't hear the Father. But the moment he conquered the grave and then ascended to heaven, they received what he had. Access to the Father will be yours through Jesus as the Holy Spirit, the Advocate, dwells in you just as he did Jesus.

The veil has been torn!

And because of that, we can take God out of every single one of the boxes we place him in. His Spirit is free to roam the earth filling and inhabiting followers as we live out the promise that Jesus proclaimed: "Very truly I tell you, whoever believes in me will do the works I have been doing, and they will do even greater things than these, because I am going to the Father. And I will do whatever you ask in my name, so that the Father may be glorified in the Son. You may ask me for anything in my name, and I will do it" (John 14:12–14). Let's be clear. This promise is not for your glory. This promise is not to proclaim that you are a little *g* god, able to speak whatever you want into existence. No. Jesus made it very clear in verse 13 that the promise is for the sole purpose of bringing glory to the Father through the Son.

Just like me, you will have doubts and questions, but I pray that as the Father proves himself faithful through his Holy Spirit, that your faith grows, your obedience becomes more frequent, and you defeat the devil by the blood of the Lamb (Jesus first) and the word of your testimony (Revelation 12:11). (The story he produces in your life will bring glory to the Father.)

The same God who ruled the earth and set it all into motion then is the same God who rules the earth today. Just like Moses, Gideon, Jonah, and Peter, you may have doubts and questions, but if you do what they did and submit to the call that God places on your life, then you will get the opportunity to participate in the most exhilarating, knock-your-socks-off, deep-dive adventure of a lifetime as he places you smack-dab in the epicenter of the BOOM!

And, oh, yeah, you may be wondering about Scott. Well, let me tell you, God has never left me nor forsaken me. His words have sustained me and have been a lamp unto my feet and a light unto my path. And the one who began a good work in me has carried it on to completion. Scott has been a part of our team now since 2017, and we are on a mission to be frontline warriors for God's kingdom as we go out and make disciples of all nations. The Lord is faithful, and the time is now. Jesus himself made the promise! It's time to advance his kingdom, so make a commitment today to not just know Jesus, but to *really* know him. And once you do, may his Holy Spirit fill you up, then overflow out of you as you go out on mission to advance his kingdom.

Are you in?

MEDITATIONS WITH ROSWELL

Where do you proverbially stand when it comes to the Holy Spirit? Have you ever considered that the Holy Spirit dwells within you, and he echoes what Jesus says as Jesus echoes what the Father says? No physical gap can keep us from the unifying power of the Trinity, but many of us have squelched the power that is inside of us as believers in Jesus. The question remains: are you in or still deciding?

10

THE REVOLUTION

"No, no, no, above and beyond."

Those words bounced back and forth in my mind as I sat on the second row of our church that evening. You see, our church, Hillside Christian, was exploding and we needed more space to allow others to come in and hear the message of Christ. Tommy Politz, our senior pastor, had just finished sharing the vision that God had given him to begin a generosity revolution: a capital campaign to encourage generosity amongst the church. If there is anything I have learned about Tommy, it's that he is all in. This man loves the Lord with everything he's got, and he's willing to do anything he can to fuel the body of Christ and advance the kingdom of God. As I sat and listened to Tommy pour his heart out and empty himself of everything, I was inspired. The man was willing to give it all up, and I mean all of it, for the kingdom. Unlike the rich young ruler, Tommy was willing to sell it all as he led the way in this generosity revolution. After Tommy wrapped up, Jonathan Mast, another pastor on the teaching team, began to share what the Lord had laid on his heart. As I sat in my chair on that second row, the Lord impressed upon me *fifteen percent.* I began to reason. I think we can do that. We are giving ten percent now, so I think another five percent is doable. Then the Lord told me *No, no, no, above and beyond.* Then I thought, *Twenty-five percent? Okay, Lord, if that's what you want, I'm in.* I kid you not, no more than thirty seconds had passed from the time that the Lord had given me that direction that Jonathan said, "The Lord has called our family to do something different than Tommy's family. For the Mast family, he has asked us to commit twenty-five percent over the next two years." That right there is what I love about the Lord. He has a knack for confirming the words he says. His words never come back to him void! I've got goosebumps as I write this because the Lord just confirmed what you read just a few chapters back in "The March." "'For my thoughts are not your thoughts, neither are your ways my ways,'" declares the LORD. "'As the heavens are higher than the earth, so are my ways higher than your ways and my thoughts than your thoughts'" (Isaiah 55:8–9). God continues, "'So is my word that goes out from my mouth: It will not return to me empty, but will accomplish what I desire and achieve the purpose for which I sent it'" (Isaiah 55:11). Rest in this truth: God's Word will not come back to him void!

As that evening service wrapped up, I asked Brandi, "Did you feel led to do anything specific?" She looked at me and without hesitation said, "I felt led that we should give 100 percent of the profits from one spec home per year."

"Awesome, I'm in!"

It was going to be a big sacrifice for us personally, and for our business, but that's what we were called to do. This life is not our own. We were bought with a price—Christ's sacrifice—therefore our lives (and possessions) are not our own. I've always said, "Lord, this is yours. My hands, they are open. My feet, they are willing to move. You direct my path, and I will follow you on the incredible adventure you have planned for my life!" So from December 2017 to December 2019, our goal was to do anything we could to help fund the kingdom work our church was launching into, both locally and around the world.

THE CALL

February 6, 2018, my phone rang. "Hey, Steve, how's it going, man?"

"Not that great. I don't have my job anymore, and I haven't been able to find anything."

I had an idea of where this was headed, so I replied, "I can't hire you. We just stepped into a generosity revolution at our church, so I don't have anything to offer," a.k.a. "we don't have any money." Forget the fact that I didn't even show any sympathy for the guy. What a jerk I was. The man had just lost his job, and all I could muster up was "I can't hire you." What a guy.

Steve responded, "I figured you couldn't hire me, as I know you just launched off on your own with the home-building business, so I wasn't going to ask for a job. I just wanted to see if we could grab some coffee and network. I'd like to see if you know anyone who might be hiring."

As a side note, I hate coffee, but it seems like that's what grown-ups do—head to the local coffee shop and chop up what's going on in life. (If you're reading this, and we ever get the chance to meet, Bahama Bucks would be my first pick. If that's a no-go, somewhere with a caramel apple cider will suffice.)

"Yeah, for sure, man! Let's meet tomorrow morning."

You may be wondering, who is Steve, and where did he come from? I'm glad you asked. Steve and I worked together at Battery Joe during those two years of transition from the restaurant business to the home-building business. He is what we like to call Swiss Army Knife. He's done it all: church planter and pastor, florist, wood worker, concrete finisher. He started as an entry level sales associate at Battery Joe and worked his way all the way to the corporate office. He's an Adobe Illustrator whiz, former Boy Scouts leader, master of all tools, spreadsheet lover, and has the mind of an engineer. He's Swiss Army Knife.

Unbeknownst to me during the two weeks of rejections the Holy Spirit was nudging Steve: "You need to call Keith." (I didn't find that out until October 2019, over a year and a half later.) Steve thought it was to network, but remember God's thoughts are higher than ours—God had a different plan.

As I sipped on a delicious caramel apple cider, I dove right in. "I'm not sure if my father-in-law is hiring, but I could reach out to him about any marketing positions they may have. I also know Blake Buchanan at Bahama Bucks. I was going to go work there, but as you know, I stayed at Battery Joe. Let's take a look at your résumé and see what you've got going on. Where all have you looked?" Steve told me that he has been looking for the last couple of weeks and that he had had a bunch of great interviews but no takers. He needed help finding something, and he needed it ASAP. You see, Steve was the sole provider for his family of six. He had received a severance package, which was helping him work his way through the process of finding a new job, but he still hadn't found anything. And the clock was ticking.

As we were sitting there in that coffee shop going through his résumé and trying to find someone who could hire him, the Holy Spirit whispered to Steve, "Ask him for the job." Steve knew where I stood regarding a job. Steve knew the answer would be yet another no. For thirty minutes Steve had argued with the Lord. *He's already told me there was no job.* Finally, out of obedience to the Lord, Steve took a step of faith. Full of the Holy Spirit, Steve looked me in the eyes and boldly asked, "Can I come work for you?"

Now hold the phone! That took some guts! I had already established just one day before that I didn't have a position available, but remember, God's thoughts are not our thoughts. My ways are not his ways, and the words that leave his mouth never come back to him void. As soon as Steve asked for the job, the Holy Spirit went to work on me, downloading Matthew 25:35 before I could even utter a word or develop a thought: "And when I was hungry you gave me something to eat. And when I was thirsty you gave me something to drink." I didn't go into that meeting with any intent whatsoever to hire Steve—but God did. This is what Jesus meant when he said to his disciples: "whatever you did for one of the least of these brothers and sisters of mine, you did for me" (Matthew 25:40) and "To whom much is given, from him much will be required" (Luke 12:48 NKJV). Even though we didn't have much at the time, God had given us a talent to steward, and he was asking me to steward the gift that he had so purposefully laid in my hands.

In a crazy turn of events, my world, and Steve's world, got flipped inside out and upside down as I found myself asking God, *Am I supposed to hire this dude too? We just started this generosity revolution at church; what do you want me to do?* What did he want me to do? He wanted me to be obedient to the words he had given me. He wanted me to trust him. He wanted to show me that he was bigger than anything I could imagine. He just kept reminding me of Matthew 25:25, as he confirmed every bit of what he had said. For the next couple of weeks, I sought the Lord. I prayed. I journaled. I listened. I read. And through it all, God just kept telling me, *Hire him.* So on Friday February 23, 2018, I called Steve and told him that I was going to bring him on. The plan would be for him to start on the first Monday in March. I could hear Steve light up on the other side of the phone as he thanked me for the opportunity.

That weekend I couldn't shake the feeling that something was off. Something just didn't feel right. The Lord was pressing in on me to trust him and not just rely on my own thoughts or bank account. Remember, Steve needed it, and that clock was ticking. I prayed and listened for the Lord for the rest of that weekend. Then on Sunday, I pulled out my phone and called Steve again. "You know what, man? I can't shake what the Lord is asking me to do. A week isn't going to make or break us, and if it does, I've got bigger problems. Why don't you start tomorrow." Steve lit up again, and I could hear the gratitude and excitement pouring out of him. Once again, the Lord's words did not return to him void. Once again, I'd be remiss if I didn't tell you that I was scared out of my mind regarding this hire. Trusting the Lord with everything doesn't always make sense in our logical, human mind, but he had begun to show me over the years that he had a plan, and if it is his will, he will see it through.

YES, HE DID!

So what does God do next? He orchestrates and sets into motion what only he can do. He shows off. That's what he does. What you are about to read next is the order in which it all went down as God continued to direct our path:

Sunday, February 25, 2018: I gave Steve the official go-ahead that we are going to start the next day.

Sunday, February 25, 2018: Yes, you read that right. That very day, my phone rang, but this time it was not someone looking for a job; it was a potential client looking for a new home.

Sunday, February 25, 2018: I opened my email, and lo and behold, what did I find staring at me? You guessed it: another potential client wanting to meet.

Wednesday, February 28, 2018: I walked into the office, looked at Steve, and said, "Another email came in last night. That's three in as many days! The Lord is good!"

Wednesday, February 28, 2018: Another inquiry crossed my desk as God showed just how mighty he is.

In just four short days, I had four potential clients that wanted to meet, and for all my math friends out there, you are correct, that equates out to an average of one inquiry per day. Prior to hiring Steve, I was getting maybe one or two inquiries per month! The Lord was at work, and he was going to provide our every need. Now here is what you have to understand. We wouldn't be able to touch much of that money for several months, but this is what God was telling me: "Follow me, and if you put your trust in me and are obedient to my call, I will sustain you. I will meet your every need."

MANIPULATION OR OBEDIENCE?

So how do we know the difference between manipulation, a.k.a. prosperity gospel, and obedience? How do we, as followers of Christ, differentiate the two? Jesus gives us the answer in Matthew 7:15–20. It's by our fruit. So when someone tries to manipulate God, it is for their benefit and for their glory. Obedience, on the other hand, is dying to your own agenda—your own kingdom, your own glory—as you submit to the King of kings with the sole purpose of bringing glory to his name. Manipulation of God says, "I'm going to do this so God will give me that." Obedience, on the other hand, says, "God asked me to do this and even though there may be challenges—even if it may be difficult—I'm going to do what he asked me to do, and I'm going to do every bit of it for his glory!" As I said in the last chapter, God isn't some magic genie here to grant your every wish. Remember, he is the God of the universe, the King of kings, the Great I Am, and he is allowing us to participate and partner with him as he advances his kingdom. Let's not get it twisted—as we so often do—and allow our culture to completely flip these roles around. All too often, we are after the advancement of our agenda and call on God to partner with us as we try to advance our own kingdom rather than the other way around.

I pray that you don't fall into the trap of trying to manipulate God. If you do take that route, you're going to find yourself empty. Instead, I pray that you would allow God to be your potter, your maestro, your King, your everything as you lay down your life in complete submission and obedience as you advance his kingdom. His Word will never come back to him void, so I pray that you will pursue him with everything you've got as you listen intently for a word from him. You may be thinking to yourself, *this is all great, but how do I hear from God?* First, instead of saying, "God, do this, or God, do that for me," start saying, "God, what can I do for you today?" Then, be quiet and listen for that still, small voice of the Holy Spirit. *What if I don't hear him?* you might ask. Keep praying! Get into his Word. Seek out others who are hearing from him. For me, fourteen years passed from the time I had accepted Christ to the first time I heard his voice. So don't give up!

Maybe you are thinking *What about the Lord's Prayer? Didn't Jesus pray to his Father: 'Give us this day our daily bread.' Wasn't that about his needs?* He sure did, but like I said in the last chapter, we can't just cherry pick Scripture and use it how we want. We can't look at that part alone; we have to look at the whole. Jesus came to this earth to advance his Father's kingdom. As the perfect, sacrificial atonement, he laid down his life for a wicked and wretched world. As you study Christ's teaching, and look at the whole of his message, it was for one purpose: to advance his Father's kingdom. If we understand that to be gospel truth, then let's look at what he's teaching the twelve disciples regarding prayer, while at the same time considering his mission to advance his Father's kingdom. Let's break it down request by request.

"Give us this day our daily bread" so that we can advance your kingdom.

"Forgive us of our trespasses as we forgive those who trespass against us" so that we can advance your kingdom.

"Lead us not into temptation but deliver us from evil" so that we can advance your kingdom.

In other words: fill us up as you provide for our daily needs, give us grace so that the grace we experience can overflow out of us and into others, and keep us from any temptation or evil. Why? *So we can advance your kingdom!* Jesus was teaching us to die to our own agenda—our own selfish prayers—as he modeled how to pray with obedience so his

Father's kingdom could come and his will could be done on earth as it is in heaven. It's time to die to our own manipulative, selfish prayer tactic and humbly submit ourselves at the foot of the throne in complete and submissive obedience.

As I wrote this chapter, God began to reveal things about my own story—my own journey. In order for me to hear the voice of the Lord, I had to die to my agenda. I had to die to my habit of trying to manipulate God. I had to break away from a Western culture that says to focus on me, me, me and die to my own kingdom. Don't wait! Don't wait until your life is hanging by a thread and you're at the end of your rope. Instead, lay down your life and die to your agenda as you drop your nets and follow Jesus.

When you first opened this book, I told you it wasn't about me. As you continue to read this story, you're going to see the beauty of that statement begin to unfold. Steve had to be hired, and what's more, he had to be hired when the Lord had said to do so. Why? Because his words never return back to him void. The God of the universe, the God of the angel armies was at work, and he was orchestrating one crazy, wild goose chase of an adventure with one purpose in mind, and one purpose only:

Finding you.

MEDITATIONS WITH ROSWELL

God's economy is different—sometimes seemingly weird and incredibly difficult to keep up with. Mostly because God's plans are literally out of this world! Nevertheless, he mandates generosity. And as we grow in generosity, ironically, we grow in humility and obedience. Was there ever a time that God called for you to be generous? Do you hold any barriers to generosity? If so, what in your life has created those barriers?

11

THE THEORY

I can't tell where we were or what we were doing, but I can tell you that Brandi looked me dead in the eye and said, "You've got to start working out." Was I starting to look bad? Maybe it's because I was showing some signs of stress or grumpiness, and she knew working out would release some much-needed endorphins into my body. Regardless, one thing was certain: she was right. I needed to work out. Herein lay the problem, though. Every time I got pretty serious about working out again, it's like my body would fight back and tell me, *nope, we ain't doing that again. You, sir, have put us through enough already.* Growing up, I never gave my body a break. Like ever. Starting at the age of three, it began with soccer. From that point on, if there was a ball involved, or a chance to win, you could guarantee yourself that you'd find me there. Soccer, baseball, basketball, football, and track were all my jam, so needless to say, I put my body through a lot. I've got a compressed disc and bone spurs in my back, a partially torn meniscus, and tendonitis in my shoulder and hamstring—everlasting trophies from my all-out pursuit of the games I loved.

"You're right," I said, "but every time I go back to the gym, I wind up laid up in bed or hurting myself again." I remember a specific bout where I went toe to toe with my back, and let me tell you, my back won by knockout. It wasn't even close! For three days I was stuck in bed. I could hardly move, and standing up wasn't even an option. The only thing I could do was slowly lower myself out of bed, get on all fours, and crawl to the bathroom and back. It was brutal.

Not willing to take no for an answer Brandi replied, "Why don't you go try Orangetheory?"

"I'm not going to Orangetheory. First of all, that's a woman's place. Second of all, I lift weights. Third, that's group fitness, so go back to point number one: that's a woman's place."

Brandi listened to the excuses and the pride oozing out of my mouth and then said, "Oh, get over yourself. The first class is free, so if anything, just go get a workout in and put your body to the test."

Full of pride, I said, "Fine! I'll go do the workout, but I'm not going to sign up."

I wasn't sure which was worse for my back—my compressed disc or my lovely wife being all up on it. One thing was certain, I was determined to fix one of my two back problems. It was time for Brandi, my beautiful, lovely wife, to get up off my back. I signed up to go to my first free class on April 30, 2018, and by May 1, not only was I a premier member with unlimited access, but I was in talks with the area representative about opening a location in San Angelo, Texas. You read that right. After just one class I found myself back in my truck googling "Orangetheory Franchise." Let's take a quick pause. I've got to go ahead and get this over with. Brandi, you were right. It's on the record. You, my beautiful bride, were right!

Orangetheory was now my jam! So what is Orangetheory? The best way I can describe it is to compare it to the workouts I did while playing ball at Tech. While not exactly the same thing, the music was blaring, there was a coach on the mic, and I didn't have to think about a thing. It was like a party up in there. And to top it off, it absolutely kicked my butt.

But here was the beauty of that butt kicking—I really, really liked it.

Back at the house, and not more than a few steps inside, Brandi asked me, "What'd you think?"

"I loved it! You were right. I signed up to be a premier member, and not only that, I think I want to buy one."

Brandi looked at me completely dumbfounded. "You want to do what?"

"I think I want to buy one. God opened my eyes while I was in there, and I absolutely fell in love. And check this out, they have an available franchise in San Angelo, Texas."

Let me tell you a little about San Angelo, Texas. It's a city with a population of just over 100,000, and it's home to Angelo State University. The only ties I had to San Angelo was that my dad lived there for one year around 1958 while he was in the first grade. That's it. I had never stepped foot in that town, and I think the closest I had ever been to it was Abilene, Texas, which sits about an hour and a half to the east of San Angelo. Lubbock, on the other hand, sits about two hours and forty-five minutes north of San Angelo, so it wasn't like it was nearby, but I really felt that the Lord was pressing in on us to do it. I don't think Brandi could comprehend what I had just told her. I looked at her and in true Adamic form jokingly said, "Woman, this is your fault. If you hadn't told me to go work out there, I never would have done this. Just like Eve, this is your fault."

All kidding aside, Brandi was trying to recover from the nuclear bomb I had just dropped on her. Her immediate reaction was an absolute no, but she was willing to oblige my idea and said, "Can we take some time, like a couple of months, and pray about this?" Of course, I said yes, and we started walking down the path to determine if this truly was what the Lord would have us do.

After much prayer, both individually and together, seeking the Lord in his Word and listening for his voice, I was confident that this was what the Lord would have us do. He kept taking me to scripture after scripture over those two to three months confirming that we were to go, and he was sending us to a new land. Brandi was still extremely nervous about it, but she didn't want to break my heart because she saw the passion welling up inside of me as we explored this new adventure. Her prayer strategy was that if the Lord did not want us to go, he would work through the bankers as they told us no. Well, the bank told us yes, so off we went to open an Orangetheory Fitness in San Angelo, Texas.

ALL ABOUT REFINEMENT

Please don't think we were just strolling down some easy, care-free path. It was anything but easy. It has been hard. Ridiculously hard. There have been struggles. There have been doubts. I have wrestled with fear stacked upon fear, but the beauty of it all and the rest my heart and soul finds through all of it is that the God of the universe has been forging me through the fire. Isaiah 48:10 says, "See, I have refined you, though not as silver; I have tested you in the furnace of affliction." That last scripture is another one of those verses that we like to cherry pick, but we can't stop there; we must continue on and read the next verse too. *"For my own sake, for my own sake, I do this. How can I let myself be defamed? I will not yield my glory to another* (Isaiah 48:11, emphasis mine). He hasn't been forging me through this fire so I can experience some newfound level of glory or strictly for my personal development or personal growth. No! We've got to get outside ourselves. He has forged me through the fire for *his* sake, and for *his* glory! Here's the great news. He didn't stop with Isaiah, and he isn't going to stop with me or with you. No, sir! You've got to remember that he's raising up an army, so he's forging you through the fire too. All for *his* sake. All for *his* glory! You just have to make one promise: don't quit. Remember, everything, and I mean everything, is for his glory. Everything we do on this earth is for the purpose of advancing God's kingdom, and as we take the step to trust him and follow him, he so graciously allows us the opportunity to participate in his kingdom advancement. We get the opportunity to step into the full armor of God as he declares us front line warriors for the army of all armies.

The devil wants us to focus on ourselves, and let me tell you, our Western culture has done a phenomenal job of teaching us to do just that. Do you see it? Can you see through all the muck and mire to see that the real life—the life of adventure—the life of freedom—the life of following Jesus is going to take you through the fire? If you're looking for comfort and an easy path, you're in the wrong place. Jesus never promised comfort. In fact, when a teacher of the law came up to Jesus and said, "Teacher, I will follow you wherever you go." Jesus didn't throw a party. He didn't jump up and down and say, "Let's go!" He didn't look at this man and say, "I'm so excited for you to join my team. Life is about to get really easy for you. He simply replied, "Foxes have dens and birds have nests, but the Son of Man has no place to lay his head" (Matthew 8:20). In other words, he told him the animals have a place to call home, but if you follow me, it's going to be one crazy adventure. In fact, it's going to be so crazy that I can't even to tell you where I'm going to sleep tonight…or any night for that matter. You can follow me. But if you're looking for comfort, I'm not the one to follow. God has truly wrecked me on this one. Following Jesus does not equal comfort. Following Jesus doesn't make life easy. Following Jesus will cause you to be forged through the fire and then spit out on the other side refined, shaped, and molded into the kingdom warrior that God created you to be. You'll be unwavering—unshakable. I'll go ahead and declare right now, you will be unrecognizable because the God of the universe will have taken you just as you are and forged you through the furnace of affliction. The old will be gone; the new will come. And what's more, we will glory in our sufferings because we know that "suffering produces perseverance; perseverance, character; and character, hope (Romans 5:3–4). He's going to give you a testimony!

The common theme here is as the heavens are higher than the earth, so God's ways are higher than our ways and his thoughts are higher than our thoughts. Much of what I've done over the last nine years hasn't always made sense, but remember, the Lord's word will never return to him void. It will accomplish what he desires and achieve the purpose for which he sent it out.

As we walked down the road to opening Orangetheory, we were met with the reality that we were going to have to put money down on a small business association loan. Thankfully, though, our homebuilding business had really begun to take off over the previous five to six months since hiring Steve, but once again, I was torn between the down payment for Orangetheory on one side of the equation and the generosity revolution on the other.

THE DOUBLE BLACK DIAMOND

I wrestled with God as I took Orangetheory and the down payment to him in prayer. It went something like this: "Lord, I want to make sure I'm lockstep with you when it comes to opening Orangetheory. You've showed me and confirmed every bit of it, but honestly, I don't understand. Every time I turn around and am ready to help fund the generosity revolution, you throw me a curve ball and do something completely different. Now, once again, like when we hired Steve, instead of giving this money to the church, I've got to put it toward opening this studio; I'm confused. I don't understand what you're doing, Lord!" The next question that came out of my mouth is in my opinion the most dangerous question you can take before God. Yet there once again sits a paradox. On one hand, the danger is extreme. On the other hand, it's simultaneously one of the most exhilarating questions you can take to the Father: it's what I consider to be a double black diamond question.

When you stand at the top of a mountain, skis turned parallel to the edge and look down over that double black diamond run, it's daunting, but for me, it's one of my favorite things in the world. There is nothing better than the moment before you drop into a double black diamond. I love adventure. I love the thrill and exhilaration that runs through my body as my skis hang halfway over that edge. And once I drop in, it's game on. There's no turning back. It's steep. The moguls are big. The boulders present a challenge. But through it all, I trust my training. As I reflect back, it took years for me to work my way up to a double black diamond. I started in ski school when I was five years old, but I didn't just show up to that ski school and have the time of my life. It was just the opposite; I remember being absolutely terrified. I cried. I didn't feel safe, and that's all I wanted—to feel safe. As I got out on that mountain for the first time, I had so little control over my skis that they had to tie them together so I could make a wedge. As my first day in ski school progressed, I got better, and as the years passed, I got more confident. I began to trust my training. I began to rely on the teaching I received when I was just five years old. I didn't just jump from ski school to a double black diamond. I had to go through the process. I had to gradually test my limits as I took the steps from bunny slopes to green to blue to black and finally to double black diamond. Each time I leveled up, I was presented with new challenges, challenges that made me nervous, challenges that built my confidence, challenges that at times had me wondering if I had lost every bit of sanity. But once it was all said and done and I had conquered the double black, it was time to celebrate. The mountain took its best shot—gave me all it had—but because of solid teaching, years of practice, and years of building confidence, I was able to conquer everything that that mountain threw my way.

So it is with our faith. It's a process, a journey, an opportunity to level up as we forge our way through the intense heat of what God calls the furnace of affliction. We have to depend on the solid biblical teachings we've received. We have to build a confidence that doesn't just acknowledge Jesus but a confidence that is rooted in really knowing him as you declare he is who he says he is. I'll say it again and again for the rest of my time on this earth. The trials we go through aren't for our own personal development. It's not to make us stronger physically or mentally. It's not for you to get on the other side then declare that you are some sort of self-made man who did it all on your own. Nope. The trials we go through are to build our faith and help us trust in the Lord only. Then, as we come out on the other side of the furnace of affliction, it's only proper for us to hit our knees and worship him and bring him glory. Nothing more. Nothing less. We are to "trust in the LORD with all your heart and lean not on your own understanding; in all your ways submit to him, and he will make your paths straight" (Proverbs 3:5–6).

It's time to tear down the idols that we've built. More than tear them down; it's time to destroy the idols and then let God reshape us as he takes us through the furnace. It's time to do what Gideon did and get inside the temple as we cleanse ourselves of the idol of self that has wreaked havoc on our lives, our families, and our society. It's time to declare a state of emergency. The damage is catastrophic. It's time to cleanse our land of self. Jesus said, "Whoever wants to be my disciple must deny themselves and take up their cross and follow me" (Matthew 16:24). In other words, if you want to follow Jesus, the stakes are high. Not only will you not have a place to lay your head, but you're also going to have to take up your cross daily as you die to the idol of self. Now here is what I love. He doesn't just stop there. He makes a promise. He gives us hope when he says, "For whoever wants to save their life will lose it, but whoever loses their life for me will find it" (Matthew 16:25). Are you willing to die to self? Are you willing to lay it all down? If the answer is yes, and you say, "I'll enter by the gate that you've opened," then you'll get to have life and "have it more abundantly" (John 10:10 NKJV).

Are you willing to do it? Are you willing to die to self as you take a double black diamond question before the Father? You may be thinking, "What's the question?" As I wrestled with God about what steps to take regarding Orangetheory Fitness and the generosity revolution, the question of all questions left my mouth. It made its way to the Father, and four simple, little words changed everything.

"What do you want?"

That question right there is in my opinion the most dangerous question you can take to our heavenly Father. It's exhilarating. It's a double black diamond question. I had dropped in, and there was no turning back. Let's get real. We never ask that question. It's too scary. It's too audacious. It exposes us rather than protects us like our normal prayers do, but he is the King of kings, the Alpha and the Omega, beginning and the end. He is omnipresent, omniscient, and omnipotent. He's always there, knowing all, with almighty power.

My skis were on the edge and there was no turning back. I dropped in as I simultaneously died to the idol "self" and realized that it wasn't mine to figure out. I needed to trust my heavenly Father. I needed to trust what I had been taught through the Word of God. I needed to continue fully surrendering everything, and I mean everything, to him. I needed to take up my cross, die to my own agenda, and follow him. "What do you want?" I asked. God answered, and I quickly found myself on the steepest, most extreme double black diamond of my life.

And let me tell you, when God answers your double black diamond question, prepare yourself. It's gonna be big. It's gonna be steep. It's gonna be audacious. But hear this: it's going to give you life, abundant life. What did God want? He wanted me to go all in as I went all out for his kingdom. God immediately responded to my question.

"I want 100 percent of the profits from Orangetheory Fitness in year one."

MEDITATIONS WITH ROSWELL

Everything God does in us, including refining us, is to make us look more like Jesus! What are some of the ways that God refines you? Why do you think he chooses to do it in this way?

12

THE KNOCKOUT

"Deal. Just take care of our home-building business, and don't let this thing sink because if this thing sinks, the whole thing is going down." I now chuckle to myself and think, *like God didn't know.*

Those were my exact words as I responded back to God's charge of giving 100 percent of the profits from that first year of business in Orangetheory. I honestly had no idea how we would fare. New town. New business. New adventure. But the best part of it all was that Orangetheory Fitness was no longer mine; it was the Lord's. My responsibility was to steward it, to manage it, to take care of the day-to-day business as I reported back to my Chief Executive Officer, the Great I Am.

I had to hire a team, promote the brand, and inject myself into the city and culture of San Angelo, Texas. I was looking for the perfect location in a town that I had stepped foot in only once in my life, and that had happened just a few months prior. I was going to be solely relying on God, and the people that he would put in my life, to open this business. I had no choice. I knew no one and had no experience running a fitness facility. To top it all off, I had a home-building business that still needed my full attention, but this is what the Lord had asked me to do. My area representative, Ron, and his team were incredible. Ron, who was also on fire for God's kingdom, connected me with all the right people. He connected me with the right architect, general contractor, and broker as I learned a new language called franchising. As the plans came together and the construction commenced, the time was drawing near for me to start promoting this new business.

Back in 2005 I received my degree in marketing from Texas Tech University. I've always been bent toward marketing and sales. I love to see the dots connect for people as they weigh the options of whether to buy a product or not. There is so much psychology that goes into why people do what they do and why they choose to buy or not to buy a product. I've always been a fan of testimonials. Check that. Let me clarify that last statement. I've always been a fan of *authentic* testimonials. There is a difference. If it's not authentic, people will see right through it and go somewhere else. If someone can genuinely show how a product impacted or changed their life, then the likelihood of someone else purchasing the product exponentially increases. Real people, talking about real-life experiences, leads to real-life product conversions.

As I prepared my marketing plan, God began to press in on me about my own experience and testimonial. A debate raged in my mind. As you read in the previous chapter, I had made a connection between Orangetheory Fitness and my time playing football at Texas Tech. It was different, but in so many ways, it was the same. I'll say it again, the music was blaring, there was a coach on the mic, and I didn't have to think about a thing. It was like a party up in there; it absolutely kicked my butt, and I liked it. That was my experience. My real-life, authentic experience. Division 1 football is no joke, which means a Division 1 workout is also no joke. So for me to take my experience as a Division 1 athlete and equate it to an Orangetheory workout was, in my opinion, massive. And because of that simple connection, Orangetheory had legs to stand on. But there was a problem. I valued humility.

You see, I never told anyone I played football at Texas Tech. I never wore the gear around school. I never used my "status" to gain an advantage or place myself on a pedestal. Being humble after all is keeping your mouth shut until someone else proclaims to others what you've done or gives an account of the accomplishments you've achieved, right? Then once they do, you let your head and eyes drop as you sheepishly say, "Thank you," and begin to downplay the accomplishment. That's the approach I took to humbleness.

The debate raged on in my mind. Do I tell people that an Orangetheory workout is like working out at Texas Tech? I wanted to remain humble. I didn't want to seem prideful with my chest puffed out as I proclaimed, "When I played football at Texas Tech…" On the other hand, I value authentic, genuine testimonials that are the driving force behind any good product and brand. Word of mouth is by far the best marketing anyone can have, so I had to tell of my experience. What do I do? This debate went on and on in my head for quite some time. Then, in a crazy turn of events, I got smashed with a left hook. It was God who came in with that left hook, and boy, did it land. Boy, howdy, did it land!

LEFT HOOK

Why do you hide every good thing I've done in your life? Yo! That left hook from the Lord came in strong, and it hit square. It was a knockout punch! Everything I believed about humility was about to get flipped upside down. I thought humility was keeping my accomplishments to myself. I thought humility was tucking my head as I downplayed the praise that came my way. I thought humility was burying the good things deep down inside until someone else dug it out to reveal some buried treasure. And let me tell you, the world around me praised my "humble spirit." I got told how humble I was. I got told, "Keith, I wish I was more humble like you." And in a wild, twisted way, I found myself full of pride because of my "humble spirit." I was proud to be humble. Twisted, I know.

As I came out of my daze, the Lord began to rework my mind. He began to deconstruct what I thought humility was. He began to show me that there is a difference between a pride that says, "I did this on my own. I'm a self-made man." A false humility that hides everything. And an authentic humility that says, "Let me tell you a story about what God has done with my life. It's a story that as I look back, all I can say is, 'Only God. *Only God!*'" This right here is true humility. A realization that we owe it all to God.

All.

Of.

It.

He is the author and perfecter of our faith. The apostle Paul reminded the people of Corinth what the prophet Jeremiah had to say regarding our posture surrounding humility. Paul set the stage as he reminded them of their roots. He reminded them how big God is and where they came from. He reminded them that the foolishness of God is wiser than human wisdom, and the weakness of God is stronger than human strength (1 Corinthians 1:25). Then, Paul makes the declaration of all declarations: "It is because of him [God] that you are in Christ Jesus, who has become for us wisdom from God—that is, our righteousness, holiness, and redemption" (1 Corinthians 1:30). But once again, we can't stop there. We have to read the next verse where Paul makes that bold declaration I alerted you to earlier. He reminded the people of Corinth what Jeremiah had to say in Jeremiah 9:24: "Therefore, as it is written: 'Let the one who boasts boast in the Lord.'" It's not us! It is because of *God* that you are in

Christ Jesus, who has become for us wisdom from God—that is, our righteousness, holiness, and redemption. Therefore, if you are going to boast, *boast in the Lord!*

TALENTS

I love the Holy Spirit. In fact, I'd like to say that he has become a best friend of mine as he has led me through God's holy Scripture to reveal just who God is. He's broken down religious walls, and he's destroyed a Western culture mentality that's rooted deeply within me. Through it all, he has set me free to roam the kingdom of God. I'll never forget the day when God led me to the parable of the talents (Matthew 25:14–30). In it, Jesus is talking about money, but if we look at the teaching of Christ, we have to recognize that his parables had layers stacked upon layers within what he taught. After all, Jesus is the Son of God. He came to this earth and destroyed so much of what the people of that time knew and believed about his Father. In the greatest sermon ever, the Sermon on the Mount, Jesus told the people that he didn't come to abolish the law, rather, he came to fulfill the law. There are ten simple words that Jesus says during this sermon that changed everything and destroyed their cultural beliefs as he took a deeper look at what they saw on the surface. Those ten simple words were, "You've heard that it was said _____ But I tell you _____." He then took the command to a much deeper level. It was during this sermon that Jesus says, "You have heard that it was said, 'You shall not commit adultery.' But I tell you that anyone who looks at a woman lustfully has already committed adultery with her in his heart" (Matthew 5:27–28). He then does the same thing with murder.

As we allow the Holy Spirit to lead us through Scripture, Jesus is going to take us deeper into his teaching. Remember, the Holy Spirit doesn't speak on his own accord. He speaks only what he hears from Jesus. Jesus doesn't speak on his own accord either. He speaks only what he hears from the Father. This is the beauty of the Trinity. As I dove into the parable of the talents, the Holy Spirit showed me a golden nugget when he whispered, "Change it to stories." I'm going to paraphrase what the Holy Spirit revealed to me in that moment. The parable is a foreshadowing of Jesus returning to his Father in heaven, and as he does so, he leaves a great responsibility to his followers. Upon his return, he is going to want an accounting for what he left for his followers to steward. It reads like this:

"Master! You gave me five stories, and I went out and got five more stories. I've got ten stories to tell you!" The master responds: "Well done, good and faithful servant. Because you have been faithful with little, I'll put you in charge of much. Now come enjoy your master's happiness." The second servant comes along to give his report and he says, "Master! You gave me two stories. I went out and I got two more stories. I've got four stories to tell you!" The master responds: "Well done, good and faithful servant. Because you have been faithful with little, I'll put you in charge of much. Now come enjoy your master's happiness." Then the third servant comes along and says, "Master! I knew you to be a hard man reaping where you didn't sow and gathering where you didn't scatter seed. I was afraid, so I hid your story right here in my head. I knew if I kept it there, it would be safe!" Jesus then looks at him and says, "You wicked servant! You could have at least told your friend, and maybe, just maybe, he would have told someone else. Leave my presence, and give it to the one who now has ten stories!"

I was that wicked servant.

I was the one who was scared—scared of what people would think. I buried my talents. I hid his story. I wanted to remain safe. I wanted to be comfortable, but remember, following Jesus isn't going to be comfortable, yet herein lies the truth. As I've stepped out and shared my story and done uncomfortable things for Jesus, the Holy Spirit, the Comforter (John 14:16 KJV) comforted me as he advocated for me to become the bold warrior that God created me to be. News flash! He wants the same exact thing for you!

Jesus speaks three very specific sentences as he interacts with the first two men. It's important that we break those down. During my football playing days after a game, we would break down the film and evaluate what we did well and what we could improve on. We would break that film down frame by frame, forward and backward, until we had a deeper understanding of what we did right and what we needed to work on. And so it is with Scripture. God's Word tells us that we are to meditate on it day and night (Psalm 1:1–3). In this parable there are three sentences that Jesus says tell me everything I need to know about him and his view of us. It does not matter that one had five talents and the other, two. He's not comparing you to someone with more or someone with less. In fact, we should "not compare ourselves with each other as if one of us were better and another worse. We have far more interesting things to do with our lives. Each of us in an original" and, might I add, created in the image of God (Galatians 5:25–26 MSG). He is asking you to focus on him as you step out in obedience to steward the talents, or stories that he's entrusted to your care. It doesn't matter how much you have or how little you have. All he wants is your obedience! He wants your story! He wants you to run to him as you proclaim, "Master! You gave me _____ stories, and I went out and got _____ more stories to tell you!" And when you do, his response to your obedience will be these three simple sentences: "Well done, good and faithful servant. Because you have been faithful with little, I'll put you in charge of much. Now come enjoy your Master's happiness."

It's time to enjoy your Master's happiness! It's time to share your story as you humbly submit and say, "Only by you, Lord. *Only by you!*" Ah, here is the beauty of Scripture. In doing so, you will fulfill Revelation 12:11. You will have defeated the devil by the blood of the Lamb (Jesus) and the word of your testimony (your story).

Our testimony, our story, terrifies the devil. It's why he has convinced Christians that "humility" is tucking our head as we play off the praise that comes our way. I thought humility was burying the good things deep down inside until someone else dug them out to reveal some buried treasure. Then, and only then, would I acknowledge what they found. At the same time I would dismiss the talents the Lord had given me. It makes me sick! Do you see it? Don't be like me. Don't be like the wicked servant and bury your talent. Instead, humbly submit yourself to the throne, share your story, and let yourself revel in the truth as you enjoy your Master's happiness. The devil wants to hold you back as he places the cage called "false humility" around you. Jesus, though, Jesus is ready to break those chains himself and bust you out of that nasty, old cage called "false humility," but here is the key to it all...Jesus holds the key—in fact, he doesn't just hold the key, **he is the key**.

I hope and pray that Jesus will do with you what he did with me. I pray that he sets you free as he breaks those nasty, old chains. Freedom! Freedom to roam his kingdom—freedom to live an abundant life, to remove the chains of religion that bind so many of us—as the Holy Spirit whispers the truth of God's Word in your ear. It is by God, and only by God, that

Jesus finally busted me out of that nasty, old cage. I now have the divine privilege of resting in the arms of my Master as he whispers in my ear, "Well done, good and faithful servant. Well done."

You want to know the craziest thing about the whole Orangetheory deal? It wasn't just the fact that we were called to give 100 percent of the profits. Now, don't get me wrong, that was massive calling to trust the Lord. But the reality is that on this earth, money will come, and money will go. God had so much more planned that my mind couldn't even comprehend what he was doing. He was creating a testimony for me—a testimony that only he could orchestrate about his goodness, one that would leave people speechless as I told of the majesty of the King of kings. It was a testimony that would leave the devil defeated as he witnessed the power and authority of the Great I Am.

Here is the craziest thing surrounding Orangetheory Fitness: it's the simple question I get over and over, and it goes something like this: "How in the world did you get to San Angelo, Texas, to open an Orangetheory Fitness?" Before I give the answer to that question, you must understand that the Lord had given me a talent, but this time, once I received that talent, I made a commitment that I would no longer bury my story like that wicked servant. I wasn't turning back to that old man and hiding my story any longer. I was going to be like the other two guys—those two faithful servants. Yes! I was going to be like those guys.

I would no longer bury my story deep in my mind to keep it safe but would share it so that I could report back to my Master and hear him whisper, "Well done, good and faithful servant. Because you have been faithful with little, I'll put you in charge of much. Now come enjoy your Master's happiness."

Ah, yes, the question. I love the question surrounding Orangetheory Fitness because the answer to that question always starts like this: Oh, man, I'm so glad you asked. Buckle up because I've got one wild and crazy story to tell you.

You see, God...

MEDITATIONS WITH ROSWELL

How would you define stewardship? Make a list of some examples, good or bad, that God may have placed in your life of stewardship. Based on your understanding of the Bible, why would God create such a baseline or paradigm of stewardship for us in this life?

PART 2

THE CALL

13

THE SLAVE

God never called you into business to be a slave to that business.

Ever.

Not ever.

He called you into business to advance his kingdom.

This is it for today. Stop right here, and read no further.

Let God speak to you as you process what you've just read. I want you to sit in the King's presence and evaluate your life for the next twenty-four hours as you allow him access into your business and your life. Come back tomorrow with a fresh set of eyes and hopefully with a new perspective as you dive back into chapter 14.

MEDITATIONS WITH ROSWELL

This chapter falls in the "top 3" of this entire book. No questions, rather a few statements to ponder and pray through:

*God has called me to be free, in every way. That is my identity.

*Slavery is the highest form of bondage.

*In Christ, I am a son/daughter not a slave.

14

THE QUESTION

It was another hot summer day—July 27, 2019, to be exact. I was stepping onto a bus that would take me to Glorieta, New Mexico, but little did I know that God had a divine appointment set for that day. This one, though, would be between us—God and me, that is. I just didn't know it yet.

You've now joined Patrick and me back on that bus, packed with forty kids, headed to Glorieta, New Mexico for church camp. The Lord has been blowing Patrick's mind left and right as I share the talent that the Lord had placed in my hand. I was six months into that first year of stewarding Orangetheory Fitness when I found myself sharing this story with him. I had no clue how that first year of Orangetheory would turn out, but I had found my confidence in this: God was leading the charge. One of the first thoughts I had after the Lord had asked me to give him 100 percent of the profits was this: I bet the Lord is going to blow the doors off this place. I mean every bit of it is his, so why wouldn't he? But let me tell you, my confidence was much less evident on January 24, 2019 than it was on July 27, 2019, sitting in that seat. You see, on January 24, there was a moment where I began to question if I heard the Lord correctly. When we opened that Orangetheory on January 25, the way I saw it on January 24 was that we were only halfway to our break-even membership number. Doubt began to kick in. I asked God, *Did I hear you right? I thought you were going to blow the doors off this place.* For the first time on this journey, I began to question whether I had heard God's voice clearly. I began to question whether I had conjured up this whole idea surrounding Orangetheory in my mind. Honestly, I began to question everything. *You and I both know that if this thing sinks, the whole ship is going down. I was certain that this is what you wanted us to do, but I'm a little shaky about what's happening right now. Did I hear you right, Lord?* I can now laugh at myself when I think back on that question and the doubt that overtook my mind. I laugh because when I signed up for this deal with the Lord, I had been a member for only one day, so I didn't fully comprehend everything that would happen over the next six to seven months as we launched this new business. Yes, I created pro formas. Yes, I studied the market. Yes, I had done months and months of digging as I asked question after question. But what I didn't fully comprehend as I ran the numbers is just how many heart rate monitors and how much gear we would sell. I didn't calculate the fact that because of another man of God, Beau, our broker, we wouldn't pay rent until May of 2019. I didn't calculate fully that for the first six months we would make interest-only payments on that loan we received from the bank. And most importantly, at that time, I didn't fully understand Isaiah 55:11 that tells us that the Lord's Word will never return to him void but will go out and fulfill the purpose for which he sends it out. The Lord's word was "Go." My job was to be obedient to that call and let him take care of the rest as he sent his word out to fulfill his purpose.

As we got to the end of that first month of business, I peeked into the bank account not completely sure what I would find, but in a beautiful turn of events, there was money sitting in the account. We were profitable. You read that right. Profitable. There wasn't a bank vault full of money, and the storehouse wasn't overflowing. No, there was just a little bit, but God was taking care of us. He was sustaining us as he met our needs. The second month came and went. Profitable. Again, not by much, but he was getting our team acclimated as we worked together to figure out the flow and systems of this new business. God, true to form, ordained it all. He set this meeting into motion years before that July 27, 2019, bus encounter. Everything that you've read up to that point led to this divine appointment that would have me colliding with the God of the universe on that bus. As Patrick took it all in, eyes wide open and mind fully blown, I had one more story to share with him before the Lord would grab me by the arm and take me on a journey that would change everything.

As I sat on the floor of that studio surrounded by our newly hired staff, I began to lay out a vision to the very ones who would execute and deliver on what the *New York Times, The Today Show*, and so many other major publications had declared, "The best one-hour workout in the country." I needed them to fully comprehend how incredible this workout really was. These were going to be the people with boots on the ground as we opened our doors to the people of San Angelo, Texas. But before I shared any of that, I needed them to know some things about me. I needed them to know who I was and what I was all about. I needed them to know my background. I needed them to know the truth of who I was.

"First and foremost before we get into anything else," I began, "I want you to know that faith is a huge part of my life. You're just going to hear Jesus come out of me. For me, this place is a ministry. We just happen to provide a place where people can work out. You will have people walk through that front door that are broken. They are down on themselves because they have lost confidence in who they are. Maybe they are overweight. Maybe they look great but are deeply depressed because of circumstances outside of their control. Whoever it is that walks through those doors, I want you to encourage them. I want you to love them. And if you feel led to pray with them, go for it." I continued telling them about me, my wife and kids, my home-building business, how incredible this workout is, and how it changed my life. I didn't share with them that the Lord had asked for 100 percent of the profits—it wasn't time for that yet—but I wanted them to fully wrap their heads around the vision the Lord had given me as we launched Orangetheory Fitness in San Angelo, Texas.

Patrick looked at me and said, "I absolutely love that! I'm so encouraged by your story. To see how the Lord has moved in your life is incredible." He turned back around in his seat, and I found myself sitting in silence for just a few moments before this divine appointment with the God of the universe commenced.

"How do we get other people to share their faith like that?"

It was a simple question, but like a computer, the Lord began to download new software in me as he simultaneously asked that question. My mind went berserk. All I had said is, "Faith is a huge part of my life, so you're just going to hear Jesus come out of me. For me, this place is a ministry. We just happen to provide a place where people can work out." For years I had said the same thing about my home-building business: "We just happen to build homes." But now the Lord was ready for something different—something new. The Lord was ready to launch! I began to process what he had just asked me, and my mind immediately went to the corner of my brain called marketing, ideas, and audacious dreams.

What if we had one of those rubber bracelets, a shirt, or a hat with some acronym that could serve as a way of sharing our faith or a reminder of the commitment we've made to the Lord? Over the next couple of days, I contemplated what that word would be. I tossed around several ideas, but I knew it needed to be simple, yet powerful. Finally, I thought of the word BAM, and immediately those three little letters turned into Business as Ministry.

I was ready to roll! I quickly grabbed my phone and sent a text to Steve. "Dude, check this out! I feel like the Lord is putting us on a mission to wake up a generation, and I can't shake it. I came up with the acronym BAM, Business as Ministry. What do you think?" I then jumped onto Google and began a search: "What does the Bible say about business?" And lo and behold, what came up first? You guessed it, Bible verses about money. Bible verses about how God wants to bless us abundantly. Bible verses that take on the approach that if you run a business that God is for, then who can be against you? Bible verses such as "And God is able to bless you abundantly, so that in all things at all times, having all that you need, you will abound in every good work" (2 Corinthians 9:8) and "Honest scales and balances belong to the LORD; all the weights in the bag are of his making" (Proverbs 16:11). Then there is the Proverbs that says, "Commit to the LORD whatever you do and he will establish your plans" (Proverbs 16:3). All of these are incredible verses and can teach us much, but in the context of how these verses were presented, this is what you and I can take away from those articles: be honest and good, commit your business to the Lord, and you will experience success stacked upon success as your business thrives in abundance. Seems easy enough, right?

As I dove deeper into my search, I came across several articles that implored the businessperson to leverage Scripture for their success. And if you're not in business, don't dismiss what you're about to read because it applies to you.

We have been taught, and are currently being taught, to leverage Scripture for our success.

I'm honestly appalled and quite saddened as I reflect on that last sentence. Stop and think for just a moment about what we are being taught as you slowly read these next five words: "leverage Scripture for our success." We have taken the Holy Word of God, cherry picked Scripture, and turned those words into some sort of magic show religion that will get us health, wealth, and prosperity; truly I tell you, it's a sign of the times. Let's call it what it really is: spiritual opportunism that has indoctrinated this generation with a form of witchcraft that's turned God, the Creator of everything, into some sort of magic genie.

It's an old trick of the devil. Not sure what I mean? Check it out. Satan revealed his hand when the Holy Spirit led Jesus into the wilderness to be tempted. After two failed attempts, the devil finally cherry picked Psalm 91:11–12, yes, God's Holy Word, to tempt Jesus when he said if you are the Son of God "throw yourself down from here. For it is written: 'He will command his angels concerning you to guard you carefully; they will lift you up in their hands, so that you will not strike your foot against a stone.' Jesus answered, "It is said: 'Do not put the Lord your God to the test' (Luke 4:9–12). If Satan was brazen enough to use Scripture on the Son of God himself, what makes you think you're immune to the same tactic? We've been taught and tempted to manipulate and leverage Scripture for our own success, our own wealth, our own prosperity. It makes me sick to see how the devil has twisted the Word of God to be all about us. Hear me on this. I'm not here to blame any one person. I'm here to call the devil to the stand. It's time to call out the accuser, the one who comes to steal, kill, and destroy with his lies. I'm here to turn you back to the purity of the gospel. I'm here to reveal to you what the Holy Spirit has revealed to me. It's time for us to fall on our knees, acknowledge how we've absolutely misused and destroyed the holiness of Scripture, and let God redirect our lives as we pursue him in a fresh, new way—a way that he has always desired us to pursue him.

None of the articles or verses I found in that Google search aligned with the question that the Lord had asked me. His question to me was, "How do we get other people to share their faith like that?" I felt as though the Lord was asking me to equip businesspeople with the truth of their mission. He wanted something different than the typical Internet search results. It was time for change, and the time was now. The mission was on.

Like a kid waiting for Christmas morning to finally arrive, I couldn't wait to get back to Lubbock so I could tell my pastor, Brad, about what the Lord had revealed. I was operating at level ten excitement when I finally got a text from Steve. "I love it, but I hate to tell you that Business as Mission already exists."

Crash.

I went from level ten excitement to zero in an instant. If you were standing there, you probably would have seen every bit of that excitement vacate my body as I melted to the floor. I had never heard of any type of business ministry or what I would later learn was typically called marketplace ministry. In all my years of being raised in a Christian school and going to church, I had never heard of such a thing. Steve sent another text. "From what I have found, BAM is based out of Asia so maybe we could do BAM here in the States." I wasn't sure if that was fully accurate, but I began to process it all, as I prayed to the Lord. "Lord, what do you want me to do now?" Quickly I heard the word *BOOM*. I loved the word *BAM* because it was a word rooted in action. After all, at its core business is all about action. And at its core ministry should be about action too, so I felt like an action word would do just what the Lord wanted—send people into action as they advanced his kingdom through their calling in business. I went on a tear as I came up with every possible combination of words I could think of to make up the acronym BOOM.

Let it be known that it's difficult to come up with a string of *O* words that form some sort of action sequence. I came up with many different combinations and sent them like bullets coming out of a machine gun to Steve: Business Overtly Operating in Ministry. Business Operating Overtly in Ministry. Business Openly Operating in Ministry. Forget the fact that there is an *I* word in there. I was one hundred percent in brainstorming mode. I sent a solid twenty options to Steve and his response after all that mental exertion was, "It seems forced." Jokingly, I replied, "Well, then, you come up with something! In all seriousness, I really like the word *BOOM*, so pray about it and see if the Lord reveals anything to you." The next morning as I stepped foot on the bus heading back to Lubbock, I texted Steve: "Did you come up with anything? Did the Lord give you any words?" He quickly texted me back simply:

Business Operating On Mission

BOOM! There it was. In less than twenty-four hours, Steve had so eloquently and simply put those four letters together in a powerful sequence that would not only implore the person wearing it into action, but would also help them understand that they were a part of something bigger than themselves. Those four letters would become a launching pad that we prayed would allow people in business to share their faith in a simple yet powerful way.

I always struggled to share my faith. Deep down, I'm an introvert. If you ever get the opportunity to meet my mom, she will tell you that she doesn't recognize the man I have become. Not in a bad way at all, but she would simply tell you of how she witnessed the Lord transform my life from being the shyest kid you'd ever meet into a man who boldly stands on the Word of God. Like so many of us, I thought sharing my faith meant walking up to a complete stranger and saying something like, "You need to know my Jesus!" Or, "Do you know Jesus?" Walking up to a complete stranger and sharing anything was just something I didn't do. Ever. I couldn't even find the words to simply say hello to Brandi the first time I met her, so to expect me to walk up to a complete stranger and talk about my faith was not even in the realm of this universe. No chance. It ain't happening!

When I met my wife for the first time at the sand volleyball courts at Texas Tech, my roommate, Mark, became the ultimate wingman, and the true hero of our story. As we were leaving the courts, I said to him, "Man, that girl over there is beautiful."

He nonchalantly said, "Well, go talk to her."

Apparently, he didn't know me very well. Being in front of sixty-thousand-plus people on a field playing the game I loved was a walk in the park compared to approaching the most beautiful girl I had ever seen. What was even worse than walking up to a complete stranger was speech class. Man, I hated speech class. I'd sputter through that five-minute walk through hell, carefully make my way back to my seat before I'd black out and pray that the professor would give me a passing grade. I would rather die than give a speech. The anxiety was real!

Back to those sand volleyball courts. I had no clue what to say, and I explained that to Mark. He simply said, "Come on." As we walked over to this group of three girls, I remember there being no words in this brain of mine. Zero. Zilch. Nada. All the blood was leaving my body as we made that treacherous walk. At some point, I did begin to wonder, *what's he gonna say? Does he have some sort of pick-up line he's used before? I'm so nervous.* Mark walked up to the girls and said the single greatest pick-up line of all time. "How y'all doing?" And, no, not like Joey from *Friends.* I thought to myself, That's it? That's all I had to say? That was simple. Why didn't I think of that? It was so far outside my realm of thinking and comfort zone that never in a million years did I think that would be the sentence that would put me on the path to dating the girl of my dreams who one day would become my bride.

SIMPLICITY

Like Mark's approach, God wants sharing our faith to be simple. He wants to give us the opportunity, but it's up to us to open our mouth and tell of the goodness of our Lord and Savior. It took me years to develop the language of simply saying, "Faith is a huge part of my life, so you're just going to hear Jesus come out of me." Or simply saying, "We're in the ministry, we just happen to build homes for a living." It's amazing what conversations have sprung out of one of those two simple sentences.

I knew my job was to equip business leaders to share their faith, and I was on a mission to do what the Lord had asked of me.

Steve, being the Swiss Army Knife that he is, quickly went to work on a logo as we began the process of creating a bracelet, hat, or T-shirt that would allow people to share their faith in simple, yet powerful, ways. I wanted to break down the walls for those people who don't quite have the language to share their faith. What if instead of saying, "You need to know my Jesus!" we could give them a tool that someone could ask them a simple question: "What's BOOM?" They could then respond, "I'm glad you asked. It stands for Business Operating On Mission. I'm in the ministry, we just happen to _____ for a living. I'm on a mission to advance the kingdom of God through what I do on a daily basis."

To me, this was an incredible way to break down those barriers that exist between two people who may not know one another. Now, instead of wondering *am I going to offend this person, or is this going to be awkward*, we were simply answering a question that someone asked. They asked the question, I just answered as the door was opened to share my faith. It was a fresh, new way for us to introduce people to Jesus relationally. One of the biggest challenges we have seen in Western evangelism is the delivery of the gospel. It's been this awkward, transactional sales pitch rather than the very way that Jesus modeled it when he walked this earth. Relationship draws you closer with Jesus, which in turn draws you closer to the Father. Rather than force the gospel down someone's throat, BOOM is about engaging men and women in a deep meaningful relationship right where they are, so in turn, they get to experience God, Jesus, and Holy Spirit relationally!

I thought this mission of sharing our faith in a simple but powerful way was the journey God would put Steve and me on, but little did I know, God wasn't even close to being done. This was just the edge before I would drop into that double black diamond once again. I didn't know it yet, but God was about to take us on the ride of a lifetime.

MEDITATIONS WITH ROSWELL

Sharing our faith is one of our primary calls in the Christian walk. How or what are some of the ways that God has provided for you to share your faith? Are you currently sharing your love for God with anyone? And if so, what has that experience been like? If not, what holds you back? Step out in the authority of Christ and share with grace, peace, and humility the hope you have in Christ.

15

THE CHOP

The attack.

The marginalization.

The chop.

It hadn't even been a week from the time that I had received this new revelation from the Lord called BOOM that I found myself on the edge of another black diamond. This time, the Lord had something way deeper, and way steeper, than I ever could have imagined. Let's get straight to the point.

"What better way to chop off the legs of the church than to go after the one thing that funds the church?"

What funds the church? Money. What creates money in our society? Business. "What better way to chop off the legs of the church than to go after the one thing that funds the church?"

No longer was BOOM just about sharing our faith. That was simple. This was not.

This was war.

Before we go any further, let's define the church: the church is the body of Christ. Period. Sometimes the church meets in a building on Sunday, and we call this going to church. Let me be clear, that does not mean that the legs of the church are strictly limited to the gathering that happens in the building on a Sunday. No! The church is the body of Christ working in unison as it is sent on a mission to advance the kingdom of

God. In the physical realm, a body that doesn't move is one of two things: asleep or dead. The same can be said for the spiritual body. If the spiritual body of Christ isn't advancing and proclaiming the good news of the kingdom of God, it's either asleep, or it's dead. It's time for us to wake up.

Remember, Jesus commissioned us—drew a line in the sand—and told us to "Go!"

In this commission, some are apostles, some are prophets, some are evangelists, some are teachers, and some are pastors. But together, we are the body of Christ. For what reason? To equip his people for works of service so that the body of Christ may be built up until we reach *unity* in the faith and in the knowledge of the Son of God and become *mature*, attaining to the whole measure of the *fullness* of Christ (Ephesians 4:11–13). "Then we will no longer be infants, tossed back and forth by the waves and blown here and there by every wind of teaching and by the cunning and craftiness of people in their deceitful scheming. Instead, speaking the truth in love, we will grow to become in every respect the mature body of him who is the head, that is, Christ. From him the whole body, joined and held together by every supporting ligament, grows and builds itself up in love, as each part does its work" (Ephesians 4:14–16).

I quickly discovered that this BOOM thing that the Lord had given me wasn't just about sharing our faith. That was just the surface. I found myself being tossed into deep, deep waters. I didn't completely comprehend it at first, but the Lord had already begun the process of revealing this to me through the attack I witnessed on CEOs, the regulations that are incessantly placed on businesses, and the all-out attack on business. It was no coincidence. It was strategic. A strategic, well-thought-out, well-executed attack by the devil himself. Let's call it what it is: war. The devil had declared war on business in an attempt to destroy God's kingdom! He was crafty. This was a covert, top secret mission that the enemy had taken to chop off the legs of the church. No longer was this BOOM thing just a way to share our faith.

This was war.

The Almighty, the King of all kings was forging BOOM into a vehicle of transformation—transformation that could change the very way you see yourself, the way you see business, and the call that is on your life. God was going to create transformational leaders for his kingdom through one of the most hated sectors of society—business.

This was war.

Let me go ahead and address the elephant in the room so that you fully understand where I'm coming from. This is *absolutely not* about turning money into an idol. That's not it at all. However, we do need to recognize that money is a resource that provides fuel to the fire of God's kingdom advancement, so let me ask again: what better way to chop off the legs of the church than to go after the one thing that funds the church?

It was about twelve years ago that the Lord began to open my eyes to this attack. I didn't immediately see the depth of the problem I just revealed to you, but the Lord was in the process of slowly opening my eyes to the strategy of the enemy. You see, I've always been bent toward human behavior. I've always been bent toward the underlying depth of humans and why they do what they do. I've learned through this process that I'm way more philosophical than I ever thought myself to be. I truly enjoy working to understand how people come to the conclusions that they come to. Sometime around 2011 or

2012 I stumbled across an article that began to open my eyes to the enemy's scheme that was rooted deep in the pits of hell. I was not yet a business owner, but I had walked closely with my father-in-law who was. The article made sweeping generalizations and marginalized CEOs, and straight-up attacked them. Out of the deep, dark pits of hell came this article that was unfortunately shining brightly on my screen, and screens just like mine, all across the United States, and likely the world. The chop was on as the author painted CEOs as being greedy, no-good scoundrels who were only in it for themselves as they laughed their way to the bank. Could that be true of some CEOs? Absolutely. However, to paint every CEO with such a broad brush was deceptive and planted seeds in the minds of all who read the article.

I was extremely troubled and frustrated by the article's depiction of business owners and CEOs, but that was just the beginning. You see, a lot of online articles allow readers to leave comments, so their voices can be heard. And as the comments came in, a mob had formed. Close to 100 percent of the people inside of that virtual establishment took the opportunity to join with the author as they went on a crusade to destroy the character of business owners and CEOs. It's like these people had pickaxes, torches, and stones as they deployed themselves into this newfound mission to destroy and eliminate the "evil man" that sat at the top of organizations.

The comments were flying in as the all-out assault on these unsuspecting business owners commenced. I couldn't speak from firsthand experience as a business owner, but I could speak from what I had witnessed. As I looked at my father-in-law and the organization he had created, I couldn't help but see the impact he had made on the region where God had placed him. Although he employs over seven hundred people, he is the CEO of what the Small Business Association considers a small business in the restaurant industry. As I thought about the impact he has had, the more I respected and understood the challenges he faced. I engaged one of the CEO and business-burning crusaders. I simply explained that he (the crusader) could not comprehend the amount of weight that a CEO carries, and until you walk a mile in their shoes, there is no way to understand what they go through on a daily basis. If the reward for his efforts is a nice car or nice house, then that's justifiable for the burden that he carries as a leader of any organization. The crusader, however, wasn't hearing any of it. He also found himself on a mission. He continued on as a crusader in that mob that was marching down a virtual street in the desolate land we like to call the Internet.

MATH TIME: NUMBERS NEVER LIE

As I've said before, I absolutely love numbers, and I love math. In seventh grade, I hated math, but as I got older, I realized the revelation that numbers can bring to us when applied properly, is incredible. Numbers oftentimes can reveal much more than what's on the surface if we take a deeper look, so I'd like to take a journey through my father-in-law's company for just a moment. If you consider all the people that work at his restaurants and all the people who make up his office staff, he currently employs around seven hundred people. That's seven hundred people who are able to make a living each and every day—from entry level positions in the restaurant all the way to chief officers at the central office. That's a lot of people, but in all reality, that's only the surface. Let's dig deeper. Let's assume that the average family size in America is four people: a mother, a father, and two children. Take those seven hundred employees and multiply it by four and you get twenty-eight hundred people who depend on my father-in-law, in some form or fashion, to be a good steward over his business and to make wise, strategic, ethical decisions so that each morning when they show up to work, the doors can open for business and those people have the opportunity to make a living and support their families. That's a lot of responsibility, and I don't care who you are, that's a heavy burden to carry that not everyone is equipped to carry.

That's not all. Let's go deeper.

Those twenty-eight hundred people represent the employment side of his business alone. Now let's venture over to the purchasing side of his business. You see, he doesn't have his own production facility where he manufactures every single taco shell, spice, and everything in between to make his business run. No, he purchases those from different suppliers that are found within the city where his office is located, other manufacturers found all over the state of Texas, and the country. That means that sales reps, production managers, office managers, logistics coordinators, HR managers, truck drivers, line workers, stockers, and more are dependent in some form or fashion on my father-in-law's restaurants. Each one of them is part of a family unit that, in some form or fashion, depends on businesses just like my father-in-law's to support their livelihood. Now what number does that grow to as we look at this one man's impact through business?

Let's go deeper.

What about that plumber who gets called when a drain backs up? How about the electrician who receives a call when there is a short in the production line? What about the construction company that gets a call to come in and remodel the place or the call to build a new store because business has been good, and the concept took off? Is there really any way of actually knowing the ripple effect one CEO or business owner can have? In the case of my father-in-law, it's thousands upon thousands of people. And he is just considered a small business. Think about the companies that employ thousands upon thousands of people just inside of their own organization? Think about that multiplication effect. Is it tens of thousands?

Then there are taxes. Let's talk about taxes. We haven't even looked at the insane amount of taxes paid out to the city, county, state, and country by these companies. Through taxes, these companies have helped build infrastructure and helped support services that every single person in that region enjoys. Employment tax, property tax, franchise tax, sales tax, Social Security, personal income tax, etc., are all garnered from these individuals and their companies. These pioneers don't need to be torn down! No, no, no! These trailblazers need to be celebrated for taking the risk, which in turn becomes a blessing to countless others.

Let's get back to the chop: though what I laid out above is a daily reality, it's become clear that in our society it's never enough. More regulations are popping up daily from local municipalities. The government at the state and national level demands more and more taxes out of these people. Hate from the media intensifies as the onslaught against business ramps up all the more.

Chop.

Chop.

Chop.

Instead of being celebrated for every single thing that they do, and how much they contribute to the greater good of society, they have been flogged, beaten, and purged. We gotta take a minute and stop right here. We need to call a timeout and take a second to reflect. Remember, these people are merely human. These people have real emotions, real feelings, and real fears. Are they tougher mentally than most? Do they have a thicker skin and a longer landing strip than most?

Do they have a deeper root system to take the beatings and the chopping that comes their way? In most cases, I would venture to say yes, but at a certain point, they may decide enough is enough. The chopping will have finally cut these giant redwoods of people down. They decide it isn't worth it any longer. Maybe they make the decision to stop expanding, which brings an end to new jobs. Maybe they make the decision to close up shop and shut their doors. They think to themselves, *Enough is enough*. Then what? In my father-in-law's business, if he decides to shut it all down, seven hundred people are left without a job, but again, that's just the surface of a deep, deep ocean of impact. Thousands of people are left to pick up the pieces as they wonder, *What's next?*

Let's get away from the surface and recognize what's really happening here. Jesus told the people "The devil comes only to steal and kill and destroy (John 10:10). Paul tells the people of Ephesus, and us today, to "put on the full armor of God, so that you can take your stand against the devil's schemes. For our struggle is not against flesh and blood, but against the rulers, against the authorities, against the powers of this dark world and against *the spiritual forces of evil in the heavenly realm*" (Ephesians 6:11–12, emphasis mine). Paul then says it again in verse 13, "Therefore put on the full armor of God." It's important! Remember in chapter 7, "The March," where you found yourself in his armor room? This is why. This is what it's all about! When I said in chapter 1 that this book was about finding you, this is why. It's time for you to understand your identity and your purpose. I'll go even deeper into this in the next chapter, but you have to understand that if we go into battle with the enemy unprepared and unprotected, we are sitting ducks—an easy target. We will not prevail! But if we armor up, then "when the day of evil comes, you may be able to stand your ground, and after you have done everything, to stand" (Ephesians 6:13). It's time to stand up against this covert, evil scheme and see that the enemy's attack on you and your business is spiritual. As bottom lines erode and more regulations are put on business, the tighter everything gets. In turn, this means more often than not you will find yourself chained to that nasty fence.

What better way to chop off the legs of the church than to go after the one thing that funds the church? If the enemy can tighten everything up, then the tithe or charitable giving begins to erode. Let's be honest, I'd venture to say that the first thing cut from people's personal budgets are the tithe or charitable giving. If faced with the choice of putting food on the table to feed their family or giving to God's kingdom, I think it's a safe assumption that the great majority would meet their physical needs. At one point, that was the story of my household.

As I reflect on this tactic of the enemy, I marvel at the fact that God gave this to me in August of 2019—merely seven months before COVID put its assault on the world. And as I write this today, we are still in the process of stepping out of that pandemic that destroyed businesses all over the world, strapped them financially, destroyed our supply chain, and drove inflation to levels that this generation has never seen. Gas, food, clothing, building supplies, you name it, have all exponentially increased in price. So not only does that instill fear and doubt in people, but it's also ground zero of the erosion of the tithe. Sadly, due to inflation, those who do continue to tithe have found their tithe having less impact than pre-pandemic, pre-inflation levels. **This is spiritual warfare.**

SOUTH AFRICA TO LUBBOCK

In 2020 God divinely connected me with a man named Kobus Grobler when he showed up to our monthly luncheon in March of that year. Kobus is the CEO of an organization called Emit Global, which is currently working fervently for God's kingdom in nineteen countries across the continent of Africa. Some may say it was a coincidence, but I don't believe in coincidences. It was a divine appointment that the Lord had set months or years in advance. How does a man from South Africa just happen to show up to a luncheon in Lubbock, Texas, on the first Tuesday of March (the day God led us to set for the event), just fifteen minutes before we had our monthly BOOM luncheon?

Not a coincidence.

Didn't just happen.

It was God ordained.

What's more, God had much more for us than for him to just show up to our luncheon. This was a divine appointment, remember? As Kobus sat across the table from me a mere two days later, he looked at me and said, "I was so inspired by what you had to say on Tuesday. You see, God has us on the same mission in Africa, raising up business leaders and young men for the kingdom of God."

Not a coincidence.

Didn't just happen.

It was God ordained.

The only way I can describe the relationship between Kobus and me is what I like to call unity of the Spirit. It's like Kobus and I had known each other our whole lives. It was wild! As I continued my conversations with Kobus, he gave me a stat—a sobering stat. He told me that 60 percent of all money that funds global missions originates in the United States. On the flip side, that means that the other 40 percent comes from the remaining countries across the globe. According to Kobus, and backed by the National Congregational Study Survey, there are an estimated 380,000 churches in the United States. Now check this out, on average just 4 percent of the church budget goes beyond their four walls to impact global missions. That means that the 60 percent of giving that comes out of the United States alone is generated from a mere 4 percent of American church budgets. It's mind-boggling, and, quite frankly, sobering. If we truly stand in agreement with Christ to go make disciples of all nations, then we must also fund those doing his kingdom work globally. If we could get that number from 4 percent of the budget to 8 percent, stop and think of the impact that can be had for God's kingdom. We'd instantly double America's impact in global missions. Now let it be known, God is a God of multiplication. He turned five loaves and two fish into a feast that fed five thousand, and that didn't even include the women or children! He doesn't need much to make an impact, but just like that young boy with the five loaves of bread and two fish, we must be willing participants. We have to show up! If you are a church leader reading this, prayerfully consider how your church can partner with organizations who are actively participating in God's global kingdom work. If you aren't sure where to start, let me give you three organizations that are near and dear to my heart: Emit.Global, Empower-one.org, and IllumiNations. bible. Each one of these is on a mission to advance the gospel into the unreached parts of the world including the 10/40 window. Please take a few minutes to explore the websites listed above, so you can learn more about what each one of these organizations you are passionate about. Are we truly serious about every tongue and every nation (Romans 14:11) or is it just all talk?

Back to you, Mr. or Mrs. Businessperson. Can you see it? Can you see the spiritual warfare that rages over your business? Can you see the schemes of the devil as he attempts to chop off the legs of the church by attacking you and your business? Every resource that you have is meant for kingdom advancement. Every resource!

Your calling is high, and your wiring is strategic. As we step into this next chapter, I pray that your eyes open like mine did. It's time for you to step into a deeper understanding of who you are and the plans God has for your life. The time is now. The fruit is ripe. The harvest is plenty. It's time for you to become the epicenter of the BOOM!

MEDITATIONS WITH ROSWELL

Funding is always a triggering topic going both directions. Consider your own faith as it relates to God's provision: what ways have you witnessed the forces of evil wage war on that? Why do you think the enemy chooses to attack not only churches but God's people in this way?

16

THE CALL

His name was Jeffrey (Jeff) Taylor. He was a man after God's heart, a minister for many years in the Methodist church. I didn't know him from his vocational ministry days, rather through a mutual friend, Andy. Andy had invited me to join him in a book study called Mastermind, a weekly meeting with Jeff, Andy, and a handful of other men. As we navigated our way through that study, Jeff and I grew closer. He became like a father figure to me which was a welcome gift. You see, about six months prior to meeting Jeff, I had lost my dad.

It was a tragic, unexpected accident that took my dad from this earth. My dad and mom along with some friends were on a simple weekend retreat with horses and Jesus when our family's world got flipped upside down. No one in their wildest dreams would have imagined that that's how the day would end. But when God is in control, and it's your time to leave this earth, then that's how it's going to go down. It's ordained.

THE DAY

It was May 21, 2017, a Sunday morning. I was serving communion when Brandi pulled me to the side and said, "It's your mom. She's tried your phone a couple of times, and now she is calling me. I think you better answer it." I quietly left the sanctuary and made my way to the lobby to call my mom and find out what was going on.

When my mom answered the phone, I could hear the fear in her voice as the words slowly trembled out of her mouth. "Keith, your dad's been in an accident. It's not good."

I slid down the wall I was leaning against and sat on the floor. The tears welled up in my eyes as my mom began to describe what had happened. I was trying to comprehend everything she was saying as Brandi and some friends began to surround me. For some reason the horse my dad climbed on got spooked, bucked, and sent my dad flying through the air, and when he hit the ground, tragedy struck. The paramedics were doing everything that they possibly could to save my dad's life as I made the five-and-a-half-hour drive from Lubbock to Austin.

I prayed.

I prayed a lot.

My prayer started with a plea to save my dad. I didn't know the extent of his injuries at the time, I just knew it was bad. Tears poured out of my eyes as I made my plea with God. "God, please don't let him die! Please don't let him die! Please perform a miracle!" I pounded the steering wheel of my truck as I pleaded and pleaded that God would perform a miracle that day, but as I got closer to Austin, my prayer began to change. "Thy will be done." I began to pray, "God, if this is what you want, and it's time for Dad to go home, then please take him. Don't let him suffer any longer. If it's your will, then take him home." As I prayed these prayers, I knew that more likely than not I was going to be saying goodbye to my dad for the final time.

When I got to the hospital, I found out that the impact from the fall was catastrophic. The C1 vertebra in his neck had been broken, and his spinal cord had been severed. It was an unrecoverable, fatal injury. I asked for a miracle that day. Some might say that God didn't perform any miracle, but I always tell people that God answered my prayer, just not in the way I had hoped. The miracle happened when they were able to resuscitate my dad and air flight him to Austin so we would have the opportunity to say our good-byes. I got to spend twenty-four hours with that icon of a man one last time. It was the end of an era for one of the most incredible men I had ever known, but it was not the end of a legacy—no, the legacy he was leaving behind was just beginning. The legacy he left behind was a passion for people. A passion to put others above himself—a passion to pull the best out of people—a passion to raise up the next generation so they wouldn't wander or go astray. Lord, I thank you for the incredible gift of my dad and the man he raised me to be. Neither of us are, or were, perfect, but both of us, along with my brother, yearn to leave an inheritance—not of money—but of faith for our children's children.

CREATED IN HIS IMAGE

As I worked through the loss of my dad, the relationship with Jeff Taylor was divine. Jeff reminded me of my dad in many ways, so I greatly enjoyed interacting with him and gathering wisdom from his years of life experiences. As the relationship developed, and Jeff ventured into a new business opportunity, we got the opportunity to fuel one another. If I'm honest, though, it was him fueling me more often than me fueling him. By July 2018, Jeff and I were meeting once a week after he had launched his personal coaching career. Jeff had a passion, just like my dad, for inspiring people and helping them reach their full, God-given potential, so his coaching business was something he was extremely passionate about. I could speak to multiple aha moments in my time with Jeff, but there was one moment in particular where God planted a seed that would quickly sprout and transform into a tree bursting from its branches wonderful fruit—fruit that I pray you enjoy as much as I have.

The question: "What does it mean to be created in the image of God?"

That was the question that Jeff had posed to me on the other side of the phone. I took a brief moment and collected my thoughts. "I have a few cliché answers, but…" I said before I paused for a moment to reflect on the question Jeff had laid out before me. One thing you'll learn about me is I love, and I mean I absolutely love, analogies. If you can link your message to an understood, more common concept, then you exponentially increase the odds of getting that message across.

After a brief pause, I continued, "But I'm going to take it to me as a homebuilder. When I sit down to look at a set of plans, I look at everything. I mean everything. What does the house look like? What is the purpose of the house? How are the people going to use it? I look at the foundation and determine where each footing is going to be placed so that when the house is fully built, it won't collapse under pressure. I then look at all the electrical components of the house. I strategically look at the wiring and where each electrical and AV line will be dropped into the walls of the home. I could go on and on, but when I sit down and envision a new home, I look at every single detail inside of that house and then I create it . . . in my image."

I took a moment to gather my thoughts and then continued, "Isn't God the same way? Doesn't he sit down with a set of plans for each one of our lives and run through the same process?" The Master Architect rolls out a sheet of paper, grabs his pen, and begins to sketch out a plan for our life. Notice that I said pen—God makes no mistakes. There is no need to erase, and no one else has the power to erase it. His plan for your life and your purpose on this earth is set before your heart beats for the first time in your mother's womb.

He thinks to himself, *What is he is going to look like? What is his purpose going to be?* He looks at our life and the characteristics and strengths as he sets our foundation. He then takes a look at our electrical system and wires us deliberately for the life we are going to live. He sits back and takes one element at a time as he creates us . . . in his image! And just like one of our custom homes, he shapes us and molds us into a one-of-a-kind masterpiece—a masterpiece that could only be accomplished through the vision of the Master Architect, God himself.

Remember, you are the product and result of the God who formed you in your mother's womb—the God who knows you inside and out—the God who knows the hairs on your head—the God who knows everything, and I mean absolutely everything, about you. He knit you so perfectly, so intricately, so purposefully, and just like the potter with a lump of clay, he has been shaping you and molding you before your heart beat for the first time inside your mother's womb.

You are a custom.

You are one of a kind.

You are a masterpiece!

"You know, Steve," I said one morning in August 2019, "it obviously happened how it happened, but Jesus didn't need anybody." His desk was about five feet from mine to the right. I continued, "He could have come down and wrecked shop. He could have come down and done it however he liked. After all, he is the Son of God—he is God! He could have just chosen one: Peter. He could have just chosen three: Peter, James, and John—his inner circle. But he didn't. He chose twelve guys."

The explosion that happened inside my brain next could only be described as a BOOM as I circled back to the conversation Jeff and I had several months prior. The question that he had asked and the analogy that ensued planted a seed that would germinate, break through the ground, and grow into a tree that would quickly bear fruit. But check this out, that breakthrough wasn't just meant for me. It was meant for you as well. It's time to dig in!

BUST IT

It's time to dig a little deeper and break through a Western culture mentality, check that, a Western culture jail cell, that has been placed around men and women who sit in church every single Sunday. Sing, listen, tithe. Like a regular cycle on a washing machine, it's on repeat, but this is what God revealed when he opened my eyes and said:

Bust the box.

Be a disrupter.

Flip the script.

Let's bust it! If I'm created in God's image, and he wired me for business, and the very first dudes that Jesus handpicked were not a bunch of deeply theological, elite, holier-than-thou religious scholars but a bunch of business guys, then I'm called. Did you catch that?

Created in his image.

Wired for business.

The very first dudes that Jesus handpicked were some business guys.

You're called!

This may ruffle some feathers just like it did back then, but you cannot, I repeat, you cannot argue with these men's identities. You had multiple tradesmen in the form of fishermen. You had one of the most hated guys in society, a tax collector named Levi, a.k.a. Matthew, on the team (more on the name change later). You had a doctor, Luke, following them around recording everything that they did. Why? Because Jesus was new wine, and he needed new wineskins (Matthew 9:14–17). The old wineskins were the religious scholars, the Pharisee and Sadducee—the royal priesthood—who had separated themselves from the rest of society. They were the elite. The cream of the crop. The aristocrats of their time. So what did Jesus do?

He busted the box.

He became a disrupter.

And he flipped the script on those fools!

What better way to spread his message than to go to the people who lived and worked among the people. The new wine had come, and he was looking for some fresh wineskins to pour into. He found them. Where? Down by the dock and at the city gates.

I can just imagine some of the commotion and some of the conversations that were going down as these business guys stepped into their new identity. "Man, have you heard about Levi?"

"You mean Matthew?"

"Yeah, yeah, yeah, Matthew. What happened to him?"

"He met some guy named Jesus. Matthew claims that this Jesus guy is the son of God, the Messiah, and based on what Matthew is telling me, I think he may be right. He told me that this Jesus fellow fed five thousand men with just five loaves of bread and two fish, and to top it off, there were twelve baskets left over. And, oh, this is insane. He said he witnessed Jesus raise a dead man back to life! He said it was the wildest thing he has ever seen. The dead man walked out of the tomb still wrapped up in linen after being there for four days! Can you imagine? Now check this out: not only does he perform miracles, but he also shuts the Pharisees and Sadducees down. He said it's incredible to watch this Jesus fellow leave the Pharisees and Sadducees speechless as they try and trap him with the Word of God! Matthew said that the Pharisees and Sadducees were ready to kill some woman who had been caught in the act of adultery, but when they brought her to Jesus, instead of convicting the woman, he convicted the hearts of every man that was standing there. He saved her life! He showed her, and every person standing there, that she was valuable, someone worth saving. I don't know what happened to that woman, but you have to bet that after Jesus saved her life and he told her to sin no more, she ran from that place never to be the same again. I mean, how could you not after having an encounter like that with the Son of God?"

DOWN BY THE DOCK

Down by the dock conversations were happening and lives were being transformed.

Make no mistake about it. God has wired you for business. You are a custom, one-of-a-kind person built by the Master Architect, God Almighty himself. He has strategically positioned you for this moment in history. Why? To advance his kingdom as you have conversations "down by the dock." Don't believe the lies of the enemy—the lie that says you aren't called and somehow it's only those guys who stand in the pulpit on Sunday who can preach the gospel.

Growing up, did you have any friends who were called into the ministry? When my friends coming out of high school said, "I heard the Lord's voice. I'm being called into the ministry," at that exact same moment, I got cloaked. Whether I knew it or not, the enemy already had me believing that being called into the ministry was for a select few. At the time I thought, *I haven't heard that call. To be honest, I don't even know if I've heard God's voice before. I guess my calling is to continue to pursue sports as far as it will take me, find a career, raise a family, and perhaps go listen to you on Sunday.* After all, that's what a good Christian man does, right?

Right?

One thing we know for sure is that the devil is crafty. He wants to keep you at bay. He wants to keep you chained to that nasty old fence called religion. He doesn't want you to understand your kingdom identity! I write this, because I want you to know you are more than a man or woman put on this earth to make some money and maybe give some of it away. I fell right into his trap, and for many years found myself miserable and without purpose. Thankfully, though, through an awakening brought on by God himself, I began to break loose from those chains that bound me up—those chains that kept me at bay as a "good Christian man."

SIGHT RESTORED

What I didn't realize back in the early 2000s was that my friends were being called to vocational ministry, a.k.a. day-to-day work through the church. Theirs was a calling to work as a pastor or teacher within the structure of the modern-day church. It's an incredible calling, and we see that "Christ himself gave the apostles, the prophets, the evange-lists, the pastors and teachers, *to equip his people for works of service*, so that the body of Christ may be built up" (Ephesians 4:11–12, emphasis mine). Pastors and teachers here are the ones who shepherd the flock. They feed the flock the Word of God. They lead a group of people to the truth of God's Word. They care for the flock by leading them to nourishing food and refreshing water.

Can we get real? Good. We have put too much pressure on the pastor to fulfill all the roles (apostle, prophet, evangelist, pastor, and teacher) mentioned in the passage above. We have expected them to fill every single one of these roles and then some—counselor, friend, husband or wife, father or mother, therapist, and personal cheerleader—as we sit in the pew on Sunday morning and simply consume. I'd like to take a moment to pause right here and address all my pastor friends, and all the pastors who might be reading this book. On behalf of all of us, I'm sorry. You've been expected to carry a load that shouldn't have been yours to carry alone, and may I add you have done a phenomenal job of carrying the church to this point. I marvel at your willingness to shoulder the load, and I thank God that you have because who knows where we'd be if you hadn't. Y'all deserve a standing ovation! Now, would you allow the rest of us to step up, pick up our portion of the load, and walk alongside you? My spiritual eyes can see now, and I pray that whoever reads this book has their sight restored as they step into their kingdom calling. You were never meant to do it alone, so thank you, thank you, thank you for never giving up and getting us this far. We are eternally grateful!

MEDITATIONS WITH ROSWELL

There's a common phrase that crosses our vernacular, "Image is everything." Do you believe that? What or who has your identity been rooted in? Who has God maybe placed in your life to instill some of that identity? How has your identity been under attack? Now can you see the importance of your kingdom identity?

17

THE ANOINTING

I've learned over the years that it takes more than one time hearing something for it to stick, so hear this again. The very first dudes that Jesus handpicked were a bunch of business guys, and if you're wired for business, then you are called. Let's get back to the story. Enter Peter, Andrew, James, John, Philip, Bartholomew, Thomas, Matthew, James, Thaddaeus, Simon, and Judas. These men found themselves no longer as only tradesmen or businessmen. They found themselves walking with Jesus Christ, the Messiah, the Son of God. Can you imagine? Take one moment and place yourself in their shoes. What would your life look like? What would you learn? What would your faith look like? Would you be more confident? Would your friends recognize you?

My prayer is that after you read this chapter, you grasp the truth of who you are. I've said over and over to our men in BOOM that the devil is terrified of you, absolutely terrified of you, the businessman. He knows how God wired you. He knows that you have the same DNA, the same wiring, as those twelve men from two thousand years ago—those men who transformed the world. In my study of those twelve men and my study of businesspeople, it is my belief that many businessmen have an apostolic calling on their life. Merriam-Webster defines an apostle as: "1. One sent on a mission" and 2. "a person who initiates a great moral reform or who first advocates an important belief of system." Another definition is "a pioneer or early advocate of a particular cause, prophet of a belief." I would venture to say that most entrepreneurs are pioneers—starters of new things. They go, and they make. That was Jesus' great commission after all—to go and make disciples of all nations, baptizing them in the name of the Father and of the Son and of the Holy Spirit.

Let's look at a few critical details in Matthew 28. It says that "the eleven disciples went to Galilee, to the mountain where Jesus had told them to go. When they saw him, they worshiped him; but some doubted" (Matthew 28:16–17). Let's pretend for a minute and call this a business meeting. Then the eleven disciples went to Galilee to the mountain where Jesus had told them to go as a business meeting was about to commence. The boss wanted to have one last meeting with his team but some doubted. Now wait just a second. It says some doubted. Some is more than one, and up to that point, we knew of only one who doubted: Thomas. I want you to catch that the devil had already begun to cloak some of these men. He had already begun to convince them that they were merely some business guys and nothing without their leader, Jesus. But what the devil didn't know is that the day of Pentecost was coming.

If you read this as a businessman or businesswoman, God has gifted you with a specific wiring that allows you to impact society through a business or a belief—an apostolic wiring. If you couple that with a kingdom anointing, watch out because all bets are off. The devil is not dumb. He knows this, so his mission is to keep you at bay, to make you mediocre. At your best, he wants you to sit in that pew on Sunday morning. He's okay with a pew-sitter. At your worst he wants you to cheat. He wants you to manipulate. He wants you to walk in fear as you become jaded to the call on your life. His desire is for you to be nothing more than a dead man walking. He wants to attack your character. He wants to attack your purpose. He wants you dead on the inside—beat down by the challenges you face in business. He wants to continue chopping you down so that you do not *go!*

Chop.

Chop.

Chop.

PETER, THE ROCK

Peter is definitely one of my favorite apostles to study. The man cracks me up, but I'd venture to say that Peter was the most audacious of the twelve. He was a man who spoke before he thought. A man who acted before he rationalized. A man who cut off a Roman soldier's ear. A man who was the only one to get out of the boat and walk on water. A man who proclaimed the truth of who Jesus is as the Son of God—the Messiah. A man who dove into the water and swam to meet Jesus after his resurrection while the remaining ten rowed in to meet him. I can see John and the others rowing past him, laughing as they got to the shore (John 21:7).

If you're a personality junkie, Peter had to be a seven on the enneagram scale. I'm pretty sure the man had some serious FOMO (Fear of Missing Out) as he was always right in the middle of the action. He was always ready to jump and do whatever it was that Jesus wanted. This man was bold. This man was audacious. Truly, this man was like so many of us. So how does a guy who is that bold crack under pressure? How does a man, more than likely a brazen man, a fisherman, fold to a little girl? Crumbled. He absolutely crumbled!

His given name was Simon, but Jesus called him Peter, which means "rock." But in a wild turn of events, the rock crumbled. A man who was willing to pull a sword on a Roman soldier and slice his ear off suddenly became terrified of a little girl. He denied knowing Jesus not once, not twice, but three times. Now, don't jump to a conclusion that this chapter is going to be about Peter's denial and reinstatement. While that is an important theme in the story, I'm going to fast-forward to Acts. Grab yourself a drink, get some popcorn, and let's watch this drama unfold before our very eyes.

THE ENCOUNTER

It was just another ordinary day. Peter and John had made their way to the temple at the time of prayer—three in the afternoon—when they were interrupted by a lame beggar. The man had been carried to the temple gate called Beautiful every day of his life to ask for money—it was the only thing the man knew to do. On occasion, I bet the man heard the ping of silver hitting the ground as it bounced near his mat. Some sort of hope must have rushed in when he heard that ping, but I'm sure that hope was fleeting as he thought about his circumstance and having to return to the same place every single day. As the man sat there day after day, I'm sure he encountered the same people who scoffed, ignored, or dropped him a coin.

Did you know that it was Jewish tradition to come to the temple and pray three times a day? Since this was the standard three o'clock prayer time, you have to know it likely wasn't the first time Peter and John had passed by this lame beggar. They had passed right by this man two previous times on that very day! As this man begged for some money, Peter stopped, looked straight at him, and said, "Look at us!" The lame beggar gave Peter and John his attention, expecting a coin to drop at his mat. Then Peter said, "Silver or gold I do not have, but what I do have I give you. In the name of Jesus Christ of Nazareth, walk" (Acts 3:6). As they grabbed his hand and helped him to his feet, miraculously the man was healed. He then made his way into the temple courts, for quite possibly the first time in his life, walking and jumping and praising God. Commotion erupted inside the temple courts. The people saw the lame man who had been begging by the gate for over forty years jumping up and down. A crowd gathered around Peter and looked on in wonder and amazement as he began to boldly proclaim that it was through Jesus Christ that this man was healed. "And on the basis of faith in His name, it is the name of Jesus which has strengthened this man whom you see and know; and the faith which comes through Him has given him this perfect health and complete wholeness in your presence" (Acts 3:16 AMP). As Peter continued to proclaim the truth of Jesus, "The priests and the captain of the temple guard and the Sadducees came up to Peter and John while they were speaking to the people. They were greatly disturbed because the apostles were teaching the people, proclaiming in Jesus the resurrection of the dead. They seized Peter and John and, because it was evening, they put them in jail until the next day. But many who heard the message believed; so the number of men who believed grew to about five thousand" (Acts 4:1–4).

THE TRIAL

The next day they held a trial for Peter and John. I can only imagine that everyone came to witness the showdown. I'm willing to bet that the trial was held on the big stage. On the prosecution's side:

TOO GOOD TO BE TRUE

Annas the high priest was there, and so were Caiaphas, John, Alexander and others of the high priest's family. They had Peter and John brought before them and began to question them: "By what power or what name did you do this?" Then Peter, filled with the Holy Spirit, said to them: "Rulers and elders of the people! If we are being called to account today for an act of kindness shown to a man who was lame and are being asked how he was healed, then know this, you and all the people of Israel: It is by the name of Jesus Christ of Nazareth, whom you crucified but whom God raised from the dead, that this man stands before you healed. Jesus is "'the stone you builders rejected, which has become the cornerstone.' Salvation is found in no one else, for there is no other name under heaven given to mankind by which we must be saved." (Acts 4:11–12)

Whoa! Whoa! Whoa! Hold up just a minute! Who is this Peter fellow? Was this the same man who less than two months prior was scared of a little girl? Was this the same man who denied knowing Jesus to some normal everyday people and who was now standing before the high priest, and a host of others, proclaiming the name of Jesus?

Before we go any further, let's rewind to John 18. Jesus had just been arrested in the garden. The soldiers brought him first to Annas, who was the father-in-law of Caiaphas, the high priest that year. Caiaphas was the one who had advised the Jewish leaders, after Jesus raised Lazarus from the dead, that it would be "better for you if one man die for the people than that the whole nation perish" (John 11:50). Did you catch it? Peter finds himself standing trial before the same men who tried Jesus. These are the same men who sent

Jesus to Pilate, who would later crucify Jesus, and Luke tells us that Peter stood boldly before them proclaiming that he had healed this man through Jesus Christ. Peter didn't stop there, though. He didn't just proclaim the name of Jesus. He called the religious leaders to the rug! Like a boss, he looked them dead in the eye and said, "It is by the name of Jesus Christ of Nazareth, whom you crucified" (Acts 4:10). Stop the presses! Hold the phone! Peter found his bold, audacious nature once again. He didn't just proclaim the name of Jesus, he boldly held this group of men accountable for crucifying the son of God. He then quoted Psalm 118:22, when he said, "Jesus is 'the stone you builders rejected, which has become the cornerstone.' Salvation is found in no one else for there is no other name under heaven given to mankind by which we must be saved." Peter had to have known that this could be it. By uttering the name of Jesus to this group of men, he had to have known that that could be the nail in his proverbial coffin. They wanted nothing to do with Jesus, but Scripture tells us, "When they saw the courage of Peter and John and realized that they were unschooled, ordinary men, they were astonished, and they took note that these men had been with Jesus. But since they could see the man who had been healed standing there with them, there was nothing they could say" (Acts 4:13–14).

Speechless.

The religious leaders were left speechless after they witnessed the boldness of Peter. These same men who were attempting to prosecute Peter and John had walked past the beggar for years and had done nothing. Yet these ordinary, unschooled men had miraculously healed this man and set him free.

So let me ask again, how does a man go from being terrified of a little girl to boldly standing and proclaiming the name of Jesus in front of the very men who sent Jesus to the cross? The Holy Spirit, that's how!

Let's take a journey back to chapter 9, "The Voice." At the last supper, Jesus promised Peter and all the apostles that the Holy Spirit was coming. He promised them that they would do the works that he had been doing, and even greater things that these, because he was going back to the Father. Remember, when Jesus was not in their presence, these men often were terrified. They were scared of the people, nature, you name it, but when Jesus entered their presence, all of a sudden they became bold and audacious.

Let's get back to Peter. How was it that he was terrified of a little girl and the everyday common folks who asked if he ran with Jesus? Jesus wasn't with him, which meant the Holy Spirit wasn't with him. That's why the rock crumbled. Without the Holy Spirit we are nothing more than flesh and blood, weak and incapable, but with the Holy Spirit we become men and women who can stand boldly and proclaim the truth of who Jesus is.

As I wrote this chapter, the Holy Spirit revealed something very fresh to me. I've read this story over and over and have even encouraged men with this very scripture, but I had never seen what you are about to see next. The power behind it cannot be missed. In Acts 3:4 Peter looked at the man and said, "Look at us!" Not a period but an exclamation point. He wanted this man to look into their eyes because he is going to see something he has never seen before. He is going to see the Father. Jesus said, "The one who looks at me is seeing the one who sent me" (John 12:45). The same Spirit who filled Jesus is the same Spirit who filled Peter and John at that moment, and it's the same Spirit who will fill you! When you are filled with the Holy Spirit, people are going to look into your eyes and see something different. They are going to see the Father, for "the eye is the lamp of the body. If your eyes are healthy, your whole body will be full of light" (Matthew 6:22). And when someone sees the Father and believes in Jesus, who came into the world as a light, they should no longer "stay in darkness" (John 12:46).

When you carry the presence of the Holy Spirit within you, you will be bold, you will shine brightly, people will see the Father, lives will be transformed, and if you ever doubted that you were called to the kingdom of God, let these last three chapters seal the deal.

As I said in the last chapter, God has wired you for business. You are custom made, one of a kind, built by the Master Architect himself, God Almighty. He has strategically positioned you for this moment in history. Why? To advance his kingdom as you have conversations down by the dock. Don't believe the lies of the enemy, the lie that says you aren't called and somehow it's only those guys who stand in the pulpit on Sunday who share the gospel. Let this story be the confirmation you need to help you stand against the lies of the enemy over your identity. You aren't just an ordinary businessperson. Annas and Caiaphas thought that Peter and John were some unschooled, ordinary men. Boy, were they wrong! What the high priest and all his men couldn't see is that they were anointed men. They were anointed because they had been taught by Jesus, and the Holy Spirit now dwelled in them—Christ, the hope of glory, in them. You must know that anyone who has the Holy Spirit, God's presence, is a force to be reckoned with. But remember the force I'm talking about isn't a military force with physical weapons. No, God's kingdom isn't a kingdom of this world, but a kingdom of light. It's the Light that will set men free.

ANOINTING OIL

What you are about to read next could be a book all on its own, but I want you to understand your anointing, your calling. As Roswell Smith, my partner in BOOM, and I discussed this chapter, he sent me a golden nugget. Roswell is an incredibly gifted man with a kingdom anointing. As BOOM was launching, God brought him into my life from Washington, DC—another divine appointment, but that's a story for a different time. Roswell has a way of revealing things that most do not see. He's apostolic and prophetic, a word ninja who will always drive you to the truth of who Jesus is. As we were discussing this chapter, he told me a word that God had given him some years ago surrounding anointing. He said, "The anointing is the burden-removing, yoke-destroying power of God." Read that again. The anointing is the burden-removing, yoke-destroying, power of God, and once you receive your anointing, you will no longer walk in a spirit of fear (like Peter did), but you will walk in a "spirit of power and of love and of a sound mind" (2 Timothy 1:7 NKJV). You no longer have to go at this alone. God wants to take your burdens. He asks us to offer them up and lay them at the foot of his throne as we pick up his yoke and humbly learn from Jesus. Jesus is gentle and humble in heart. Therefore, you will find rest for your souls. His yoke is easy, and his burden is light (see Matthew 11:30).

God is so kind and so generous. He has given us his Holy Spirit to dwell with us as we go through life. The same Spirit who was housed in the ark of the covenant is the same Spirit who filled Peter is the same Spirit who fills you. Our life isn't just about knowledge of God. Knowledge without action is dead—a faith that is mediocre at best. Don't live a mediocre life. Instead, carry God's presence with you everywhere you go!

God has anointed you for the world of business. He wants to reveal himself through you as you have conversations "down by the dock." Are you seeing it? Can you grasp the good work God has done in you? Your purpose in the kingdom of God is not just to be a check writer, a mission funder. No! You *are* the missionary, and your network *is* your mission field. Your anointing is to boldly proclaim Jesus, but just like Peter, you cannot do it without the power of the Holy Spirit. Jesus told his twelve disciples to wait on the Holy Spirit, but once they received him, they received power and would be witnesses of Jesus to the ends of the earth (see Acts 1:8).

Remember, "They defeated [the devil] by the blood of the Lamb [Jesus] and the word of their testimony [story], and they did not love their lives so much as to shrink from death" (Revelation 12:11). You may have to give it all up. You have to die to self. You may need to sell it all. You may have to change the way you do business, but I can guarantee you will need to get uncomfortable because when you get uncomfortable, Jesus can really begin to do work on your soul—your heart—your mind. Then your mind can be governed by the Spirit and life and peace will be yours (see Romans 8:6).

Governed means to "exercise continuous sovereign authority over." Sovereign means "supreme ruler." So when you allow God's Holy Spirit to be the supreme ruler who exercises continuous authority over your mind, then, and only then, will you find life and peace. The Comforter will take all of the uncomfortable parts of this world and bring you comfort as you step into your anointed role in God's kingdom. This anointing oil is the ultimate difference maker. You will no longer be chained. You will no longer be a dead man walking. It's time for you to be set on fire for God's kingdom as the King's anointing oil drips from your heart, soul, and mind. Now check this out: as that oil saturates, it begins to drip off of you and impact those around you. The anointing oil, the Holy Spirit, empowered Peter as he dwelled in the presence of Jesus. The same can be said for you. As a leader, when you carry the Holy Spirit, you are going to impact those around you and empower your team to boldly execute the mission of advancing his kingdom.

SET FIRE

As I was in the process of writing this chapter, God had something incredible to show me—a parable, if you will. It was a Thursday afternoon when I found myself visiting with my painter, Jerry. It was an unplanned site visit, but God had urged me to make a stop at a particular house. As Jerry and I leaned against the backside of a truck and visited about life, business, and God's kingdom, he may not have known it, but he was holding a kingdom lesson in his hands. "Look at this, Keith. This rag is about to catch fire!" Smoke began to pour off the rag as he felt it getting warmer in his hands. He had noticed the warmth, but it was the smoke that really caught his attention. That oil-soaked rag had been used earlier in the afternoon, but it wasn't until we stood around that truck that it began to take center stage. If you don't know, a rag soaked in oil can catch fire if it is not doused in a bucket of water before being thrown out. Believe it or not, we've had oily rags cause dumpster fires before. As we marveled at that rag and the smoke pouring off of it, God began to teach me a kingdom principle. In the natural world, the combination of the oil and the sun will set that rag on fire. In the spiritual world, the combination of the anointing oil and the Son will set you on fire. Read that carefully again because when the Son sets you on fire, the God-ordained anointing for your life will break the yoke of spiritual mediocrity over your life.

I'll say it again, it's time for you to be set on fire for God's kingdom as the King of kings' anointing oil drips from your heart, soul, and mind.

God's Word is chock-full of scriptures surrounding God's anointing oil, and as a follower of Christ, it should be some of the best news we ever hear:

You prepare a table before me in the presence of my enemies. You anoint my head with oil; my cup over-flows. (Psalm 23:5)

How God anointed Jesus of Nazareth with the Holy Spirit and with power, and how he went around doing good and healing all who were under the power of the devil, because God was with him. (Acts 10:38)

Take the anointing oil and anoint him by pouring it on his head. (Exodus 29:7)

But you have an anointing from the Holy One, and all of you know the truth. (1 John 2:20)

You love righteousness and hate wickedness; therefore God, your God, has set you above your companions by anointing you with the oil of joy. (Psalm 45:7)

Don't wait! Please don't wait. I made that mistake. For much of my life, as much as I wanted to be like bold, auda-cious Peter, I was much more like the lame, paralyzed beggar who found himself at the gate. My hope was in that silver coin pinging as it hit the ground next to my mat. I was a fearful man. A man who begged at the gates of heaven but never ventured beyond those gates. I was a lame, paralyzed man—paralyzed and gripped with fear. A slave to my business. A slave to a mind that was governed by the flesh. A man who was afraid to step into his true kingdom identity. But I thank God that he didn't leave me at that gate! I thank God that he picked me up off of that mat and invited me to look into the eyes of Jesus, the one true God! Then, as he anointed me with the Holy Spirit, I was set free to explore his vast and mighty kingdom. The same can happen to you. Look to the Father, stretch out your arm, get off that mat, and get beyond the gate!

MEDITATIONS WITH ROSWELL

What are some of the ways you have experienced God's powerful activity in your life? What do you believe God has "anointed" you to do? This week, take some inventory on your own personal devotion—a time for spiritual formation to examine how it's impacting your business, your relationships, and your mindset.

18

THE NAME

Two men struggling, wrestling, vying for position. Each one trying to get the upper hand. One finally took it. Just a touch, and he wrenched the hip of the other. They struggled until daybreak when one of them finally said, "Let me go." The one who had been overtaken, the one with the wrenched hip replied, "Not until you bless me." The one who brought the affliction, the one who inflicted the hip had one more question (see Genesis 32:22–32).

It's one of my favorite stories in the Bible. Jacob is on his way to meet his brother Esau when he sends some messengers up ahead of him. When the messengers return, Jacob is told that Esau is on his way to greet him but that he is accompanied by four hundred men. Overcome with fear, and in complete distress, Jacob divides the people who are with him into two groups. He then thinks to himself, "If Esau comes and attacks one group, the group that is left may escape" (Genesis 32:8). In a moment of complete panic, Jacob feared for his life as all of the deception, lies, and guilt of deceiving his father and stealing his brother's birthright rushed back in and haunted his soul. For years, Jacob carried this burden, and as you read this story in God's word, you can see that it has been eating him alive.

PARANOIA

Paranoia tells him that his brother is out for revenge, that he's out to get him, that he's coming to take back what was rightfully his. Jacob prays earnestly that God will rescue him from the hand of his brother. If you put yourself in the story, you can hear the desperation in his voice. Doubt about what God had told him sets in. God had told him to go back to the land where he was from and that he would make him prosperous, but instead a deep, deep fear gripped Jacob as he set out to do everything he could to win over his brother. Gifts are what he thinks will do the trick. I bet he thought if he showered Esau with goats, rams, camels, cattle, and donkeys, he'd have mercy on him. Maybe, he thought he'd live to see the blessing of the Lord if he could pacify Esau. Jacob sent his servants with all the gifts for Esau along with a hope and a prayer that Esau would have mercy on him and his people.

WRESTLING

That night as Jacob was all alone a fight broke out. Jacob didn't find himself wrestling with Esau or one of his men but with God. All night Jacob and God battled, and the Bible tells us that Jacob could not be overpowered, so God did what only God could do. He touched the socket of Jacob's hip, leaving it wrenched. God said to Jacob, " 'Let me go, for it is daybreak.' But Jacob replied, 'I will not let you go unless you bless me' " (Genesis 32:26). At that point God doesn't just oblige Jacob's request. No, there is something more. God needed to know something more, so he asked him, " 'What is your name?' 'Jacob,' he answered" (Genesis 32:27).

Now why would God ask that? Of all the things he could have said to Jacob, why did he choose that question?

Remember, this isn't a conversation that's being had around a nice prayer breakfast. They were right in the middle of a struggle. God has just struck Jacob's hip, and I'm sure that Jacob squalled out in pain. Even after all the blessing that was upon Jacob's life, he wanted more. He had received his father Isaac's blessing, the one intended for Esau, but a blessing that Esau gave up for a simple bowl of soup. He had finally been set free and received Rachel, after fourteen years of work for his father-in-law. He now had thirteen children and blessings stacked upon blessings. He obviously was a man of great wealth when you consider all that he had, but he wasn't satisfied. He wanted more. And what's more, you have to know that God knew exactly who he was dealing with: Jacob, the deceiver.

I can imagine the early morning dew that has settled over the land as Jacob and God wrestle. I can see God with his mighty hands gripping Jacob's shoulders as he has him pinned to the ground after touching his hip. He's ready for Jacob to submit, but Jacob grips as tightly as he can to the arms of God. He refuses to let go. "Bless me! Bless me!" Jacob cries out. For his whole life, Jacob struggled with his identity. He couldn't stand the fact that Esau was going to receive his father's blessing as the oldest. After all, he was gripping the heel of his twin brother, Esau, as they came out of the womb. He wanted to be first. He wanted to be the oldest. From birth Jacob wanted to be somebody that he was never destined to be.

TRAILBLAZER

Jacob was a trailblazer. As far as I know, when we read the story of Jacob, we are witnessing the first ever account of identity theft. This man, Jacob, stopped at nothing to get what he wanted. God knew this—he knew everything about Jacob.

God knew his past. God knew the fear that ran through his mind as he thought about the revenge that Esau must have sought. God knew the bondage and the chains that the devil had placed over Jacob's life, and he was ready to bust those chains of bondage and set him free. But Jacob has to do something. Jacob must do something first.

Let me ask again, why did God ask him his name? Of all the things he could have said or done, why ask the simple question, "What's your name?" *God needed Jacob to own his sin!* That's why he asked the question. God needed Jacob to acknowledge that he was in fact Jacob.

As the story continues, Jacob pleaded with God, "I won't let go until you bless me! Bless me! Bless me, Lord! Please, I'm begging you to bless me!"

"What's your name? What's your name? First you must tell me who you are!"

"Jacob. My name is Jacob! Now would you please bless me?"

"The chains are broken! Your sins are forgiven. Your name will no longer be Jacob, but Israel, because you have struggled with God and humans and have overcome."

God had an ultimate identity and purpose for Jacob's life, but he had to wrestle with God over his sin—over his "bless me" mentality—over the strongholds that the devil had placed on his life to receive what God had planned for him from the beginning. After years of lies and deception, the moment had finally arrived. Jacob was finally ready to step into his calling and become all that God had created him to be, but owning his sin before God almighty was a critical step toward that calling.

IDENTITY SHIFT

It happens all throughout the Bible: A man or woman appears on the scene and God completely and utterly wrecks them as he simultaneously gives them a new name and a new identity. Abram became Abraham. Sarai became Sarah. Jacob became Israel. Simon became Peter (the Rock). Saul became better known as Paul. Levi became Matthew. These are just a few. All of them received a new name, identity, or characteristic after an encounter with the living God. All of them received their new identity as a reminder and promise of the goodness of the God that went before them. All of them received their new identity as they were about to embark on something fresh—something fresh for the kingdom. In Genesis we read about God giving the new identity to Abraham: "No longer shall your name be Abram [exalted father]; your name will be Abraham [father of a multitude], for I have made you a father of many nations" (Genesis 17:5). Later, God said to Abraham, "as for Sarai your wife, you no longer to call her Sarai [my princess]; her name will be Sarah [Princess]. I will bless her and will surely give you a son by her. I will bless her so that she will be the mother of nations; kings of peoples will come from her" (Genesis 17:15–16).

What an incredible promise to receive from God, but watch what happened next. Abraham laughed at God. You read that right. Abraham laughed at God. He didn't believe it. He didn't believe the supernatural power of the God of the universe to do what he said he will do. Yet God doesn't bat an eye. He chalked it up as another human who can't comprehend that his ways are higher than our way and his thoughts than our thoughts. He had a plan for Abraham, and when God has a plan, he is going to see it through.

Let's take a look at Peter. When Jesus was first calling his disciples to himself, Simon's brother Andrew brought Simon to Jesus. "Jesus looked at him and said, 'You are Simon the son of John. You shall be called Cephas' (which when translated is Peter)." (John 1:42). Cephas (Aramaic) and Peter (Greek) both mean rock. Peter accepts this name, but it's not until after Jesus fed four thousand people that we see this come full circle. In a powerful turn of events, after Peter declares that Jesus is in fact "the Messiah, the Son of the living God," (Matthew 16:16), Jesus replied, "Blessed are you, Simon son of Jonah, for this was not revealed to you by flesh and blood but by my Father in heaven. And I tell you that you are Peter, and on this rock I will build my church, and the gates of Hades will not overcome it. I will give you the keys of the kingdom of heaven; whatever you bind on earth will be bound in heaven, and whatever you loose on earth will be loosed in heaven" (Matthew 16:17–19). I've often heard it debated on whether Jesus was saying he would build his church on Peter as the rock or whether he was building his church on the life-changing, life-breathing proclamation that Peter makes when he says, "You are the Messiah, the Son of the living God." I believe it to be the latter when Peter declares the identity of Christ, regardless, Peter stepped into his calling, embraced his identity, and became one of the major catalysts to the advancement of God's kingdom. From a fisherman to a fisher of men, Peter absolutely lived up to his name and identity as the rock that Jesus proclaimed him to be.

Then there was Saul, the pharisee of pharisees, the elite, the one who had it all figured out when it came to religion. This was the man who looked on with approval as the coats of the men who murdered Stephen were placed at his feet (see Acts 7). This was the man who was on his way to kill more Christians when Jesus met him on the road to Damascus. This was the man who attended the most elite school of its time, Gamaliel. But Jesus didn't care about his credentials. Jesus only cared about his heart and his identity, as he did what only he can do. He knocked him on his back, blinded him for three days, and then brought him to the full revelation of Jesus' glory when a man of God, Ananias, restored Saul's sight through the power of Jesus Christ. It's in Act 13:9 that we learn Saul was a transformed man—a man who dropped his old identity and became a man filled with the Holy Spirit.

Last but not least, let's look at Matthew. One of the most despised men in his time. A tax collector that went by the name Levi until he encountered Christ. Jesus looked at this man and called him Matthew. What does Matthew mean? Gift of God. Jesus was telling him what you are about to receive in me is a gift of God. Not only that, but you are going to be a gift of God for generations to come. Matthew, you don't know it yet, but you are going to write a book about my life and countless people are going to come to faith in me through the words that you pen. You are, Matthew, a gift of God!

Let's recap: We see God take a liar, Jacob, who was the first ever man to commit identity theft, and changed his identity to Israel. We see him take a man, Abraham, who laughed at him and do the unthinkable as he turned him into the father of many nations. We see him take a man, Peter, who at one point denied knowing Jesus three times, and had him step into his calling as a rock. We see him take a murderer, a Jesus hater, Paul, and transform him into the man who wrote more books than anyone else in the New Testament. And we see him take the most hated man in society, Matthew, and transform him into a gospel writer—a "gift of God."

So let me ask you a question: who are you? Will you allow God to change your identity? Will you allow God to break the chains of bondage that have been placed over your life? When he does, will you laugh at him like Abraham did, or will you stand firm as a rock like Peter did as you're filled with the Holy Spirit? Will you change the entire course of history like Paul did? Or will you remain chained up, shackled, and tied to that nasty fence called religion like so many people who refuse to let the Lord break the chains over their life? That's what the devil desires. That's his strategy. He wants you to remain right where you are. He wants your sin, your past, your doubts about the future, your comfort to keep you chained up to that nasty fence like some worthless dog, chained and harnessed, all so he can keep you at bay. Let's call it what it is, Satan wants to cancel you. He wants to make you feel like you are no good—too far gone—useless for the kingdom. How do I know? Because that's exactly what he had done to me. Remember when I said I identified as that lame beggar from Acts 3? You're about to read why.

A NEW IDENTITY

December 2019, the burden was heavy. As you've read my story, you've seen that I have stepped out in some massive ways, but there were areas of my life where I was still holding back. I knew it. God knew it. *Scared*—no, *petrified* would be the proper word to describe how I felt about what I knew God wanted me to do. Remember, when it came to my voice, my thoughts, my perspective, it was always something I hid. My shyness was a way to keep me safe. It would limit my exposure to the world. I'd always think to myself, *keep that to yourself. No one wants to hear that, and even if you said it, they probably already know that bit of information anyway.* I knew it. God knew it. So as December 2019 rolled around, God was pressing me to do something outside of my comfort zone.

I flat-out didn't know how to do what he was asking me to do. Some people may laugh when they hear what it was, but for someone like me, it was terrifying. I prayed for the Lord's help. I prayed that he would help me to navigate what he was asking me to do, and as December 30 rolled around, that's exactly what he did. He began to give me a strategy and plot a course. The next night, he did the exact same thing. He began to give me more details surrounding the strategy I would take, and as New Year's rolled around, I knew exactly what it was that the Lord wanted me to do, but I didn't want to reveal it on January 1, 2020, like it was just some sort of New Year's resolution. So on the morning of January 2, 2020, I began to tackle what the Lord had asked me to do. Before the sun had even come up, I had already begun to type what the Lord had placed on the edge of my soul. It took me three hours to write this one little post, but this is what went down:

A lifelong battle – A specific chain that God wants to break, but the grip of fear has been too strong. "What will they think?"

I'll tinker with it from time to time, even take what I'd consider as a big step, but God doesn't want tinkering, or a step here or there, he wants it all – he wants all of me. Every bit of me. And he wants the same for you.

For me, my faith has grown exponentially over the last seven years, and I've trusted God in some massive ways... but not with everything. I've held back.

I'm 100% guilty of holding back.

If you google it, it's defined as being "hesitant to act or speak." Moses fought it. Jonah acted upon it. I've followed Jonah's example and run the other way, too.

Are you like me? Have you abdicated the responsibility God has given you because of fear or lies spoken over your life? What's the one chain that God wants to break in your life, but you've ignored it like it wasn't there? How many times have you realized its presence and tried to run free, only to be yanked back by that old, nasty chain?

Whiplash.

More hesitation.

More isolation.

You know the chain. He knows the chain. Now let him break it. He has to be the one to break it!

Thankfully it's not too late, and he isn't finished with me yet. He isn't finished with you either. God desires for us to run free in his kingdom, but a giant web of lies and chains holds us back. So what should we do?

Let him break the chains.

For me, this is just the tip of the iceberg. Starting today, I'm unchained. It's time to run free and share the truths God has given me. For me, it's writing, and stepping in to one of the ways he wired me. I'm finally stepping in to the fullness of who he created me to be, and it's freeing. It's hard to step away from that fence. It's a little scary, and my heart beats quite a bit faster, but he is my freedom, and because of that, I can step out with his confidence.

I've allowed the chain of holding back to seize me. Grip me. Isolate me and cause me to hide.

Not anymore, though. Not anymore.

The post button taunted me, my heart was racing, but the time had come. I punched that button, and before anything else could happen, the God of the universe came crashing in. Once again, before I could even muster a thought, God said to me, "I'm changing your identity! You're now the challenger!" Instantly, I felt the warmth of tears running down my face. Not only had I been set free from the lies and bondage that the devil had placed over me, but God had revealed to me my true identity. My God-given, kingdom identity. For thirty-six years, I believed the lies of the devil, that my voice didn't matter, that no one would want to hear what I had to say. The devil knew my kingdom identity, and because he knew who I was, he was willing to do everything he could to keep it hidden. His goal: keep me bound to that nasty fence. I gathered myself and rested in what God had just told me and began to make my way downstairs for a quick shower. As the water poured over me, God reminded me of his cleansing—of his refreshing nature—of his truth—of what freedom actually feels like—of what dying to self really feels like. A newness came over me, and once again God needed me to know what he had done. He needed me to know just who I was, but he wasn't done yet. As the water poured over me, God whispered, "You are no longer the fearful one. You're now the challenger!"

Again, I was brought to tears, but in that moment, God took my old identity, the person I believed I was and ripped it to shreds. He was calling me to something new, no longer filled with fear but with Holy Spirit's boldness. It was time to step into my identity. It was time to become the warrior that he had always destined me to be.

SEEKING YOU

Let's go back to chapter 1. Do you remember in chapter 1 when I wrote that the whole purpose of this book, the whole purpose of my story was not about me, but it was about finding you? This chapter is the culmination of it all. Everything you've read has led to this moment. The devil— the accuser—he's actively trying to steal your identity, and let's get real, he most likely already has. You might be reading this and feel pretty good about where you are. You've got your routine. Life is good. You go to church. You're comfort- able. Or maybe he's got you convinced that you are a nobody. Nothing. A loser who can't get anything right. Maybe you are like I was and are paralyzed by fear. A man who is convinced he has nothing to offer, therefore, not able to do anything fruitful for the kingdom of God.

Regardless of any of that, I can guarantee you that the enemy has you placed in some sort of box. Check that, a jail cell—a jail cell that we can't see or feel. You've been locked up. And the key—thrown away by the accuser. So what have we done in response? We've accepted the charges brought against us. We've received precisely what Jesus said wouldn't happen when we truly follow him: comfort.

We haven't followed.

We've folded.

We've operated out of this maximum-security box called life wrapped in a dreadful paper called religion. We've thought religion was the key. Must do this. Must do that. Check this box. Check that box. Like Jacob, fear seizes us as our past haunts our thoughts and shapes our paradigm. And since this is how we've chosen to live our lives, we haven't been able to experience the full freedom found in Christ Jesus and therefore miss out on the incredible gift of the Holy Spirit as we hear from the Father. Please tell me that you can see it!

This is it. This is the culmination of all the questions I've asked you throughout this book. It's time to stop believing the accuser and start living the life you've been destined for—the life God created you for. It's time to step into God's armor. It's time to become the warrior he created you to be. It's time to bust the box. It's time to be a disrupter. It's time to flip the script. It's time to ask God who you are. It's time to die to yourself and step into your true identity in the greatest kingdom of all time. Go ahead. Wrestle with the Lord. Keep asking him to bless your little kingdom. Jacob did it. Just be prepared for him to "wrench your hip" as he brings you to submission.

The old is gone!

The new has come!

It's over!

You're pinned. Your hip is wrenched. But you've also been set free. Just like Abraham, Sarah, Jacob, Peter, Paul, and Matthew, the God of the universe has been waiting for this moment. He's patiently waiting to set you free. It's time for you to step into your God-given identity. Paul declared this same thought when he told the people of Corinth, "Therefore if anyone is in Christ [that is, grafted in, joined to him by faith in him as Savior], he is a new creature [reborn and renewed by the Holy Spirit]; the old things [the previous moral and spiritual condition] have passed away. Behold, new things have come [because spiritual awakening brings a new life]" (2 Corinthians 5:17 AMP).

Do it. Do it now! Let him break the chains and step into your true kingdom identity.

MEDITATIONS WITH ROSWELL

What makes a name so significant? Do you know the meaning of your name? If not, I encourage you to do a name study and prepare to be mind-blown. God calls us sons and daughters. How can we live in and experience that identity to the fullest?

19

THE REVIVAL

It was high noon on September 23. The year: 1857. The place: New York City. A tall businessman with a pleasant face and affectionate manner, shrewd and endowed with much tact and common sense had found himself standing in the consistory building of the North Dutch Church at the corner of Fulton and William Streets. For weeks he had passed out fliers. Twenty thousand, in fact. His desire was to partner with God as he fulfilled what the Lord had asked him to do: prayer meeting—specifically a businessman's prayer meeting from 12:00 to 1:00. This was an opportunity to come and go or spend the whole hour in prayer. On that September afternoon, with eager anticipation of what the Lord would do, the forty-eight-year-old Wall Street businessman, Jeremiah Lanphier, opened the doors to the North Dutch Church for a time of prayer. When the clock struck noon, there was just one soul there: his.

This man, Jeremiah, however, wasn't going to fold. Not one set of shoes outside of his own had shown up, but he did what he was called to do. He hit his knees and began to pray to the God of the universe. He began to pray for the people. He began to pray with a hope that the Lord would reveal himself to the world outside of those four walls. And even if he was the only one that would hit his knees that day, Jeremiah was going to be obedient to what the Lord had asked him to do. He prayed.

Ten minutes later, and he was all alone. Twenty minutes and still all alone. Twenty-five minutes and still all alone. Twenty thousand fliers. Twenty thousand fliers were passed out by this man. For just one moment, put yourself in his shoes. We've got to assume that at least a handful of those fliers went to close relatives and friends, yet he found himself all alone and most likely feeling like a failure—most likely asking himself if he had heard the Lord correctly—most likely feeling like a fool. A million thoughts must have run through his mind. What was he going to say when people asked him how his first meeting went?

The fact that no one showed up in the first thirty minutes was most assuredly a sign of the times. Money was great. The economy was performing better than ever. A spirit of mammon ruled over the people of the 1850s. People didn't need God. They had everything they needed.

Or so they thought.

So from 12:00 until 12:30, Jeremiah prayed.

All alone.

Finally, after thirty minutes, a man showed up. Then another. Then another. By the time the full hour was spent, six men had humbly hit their knees and offered up one of the greatest gifts given by God to man: prayer. The next week, twenty men showed up. By the third prayer meeting, the stock market, which had been raging with success, crashed, and the people were decimated. Now fast-forward two and a half short months and ten thousand men were showing up to pray. What better way to get a businessman to hit his knees than to take the one thing he depends on the most: money? No Longer were they meeting weekly, but daily. As their little *g* god was destroyed, they turned to the one true God, the

King of kings, the Lord of lords, and humbly hit their knees asking for forgiveness and deliverance. Story upon story began to stack up as the people gave their life to Christ. Revival spread like wildfire from New York City to the rest of the country. Newspaper after newspaper began to report on the great businessman's prayer meetings. Hearts were being transformed. Lives began to change. Businesses began to shut their doors each day from 12:00 to 1:00, so everyone could attend their local prayer gathering. Revival was sweeping the nation.

One account from the times tells of a man who had traveled from Europe to trade with an American shop owner. Once he finally made landfall in New York, the European made his way to the shop where he would trade. After exchanging formalities, he learned that the shop owner was about to close his doors in five minutes. "Why?" the European asked. The shop owner looked at the European and said, "I'm shutting my doors until 1:00 to head to a prayer meeting. I can't do business right now, but you are more than welcome to come with me." The European, now with nothing better to do, agreed, and they both headed to the North Dutch Church for the daily prayer meeting. It was at that very prayer meeting that the European man who had traveled to America to trade goods made a trade he had no intention of making when he set sail for America—the ultimate trade—the trade of a lifetime. He gave up his life in exchange for a life filled with Jesus Christ. The great exchange had transpired! With a renewed spirit, the European man and the American shop owner headed back to the shop to conduct business. Upon wrapping up their transaction, I can imagine that these men shook hands, and possibly embraced one another, as the American shop owner sent the European man back on a boat with new goods in tow, and most importantly, with Christ at the center of his life.

I want you to stop and realize for just a moment that the people of 1857 didn't move and operate at the same speed at which we move and operate today. Today, a man crossing the Atlantic to do business in America will have boots on the ground in approximately eight hours when he boards a plane from Europe to New York City. In 1857, the Wright brothers weren't even born yet. That first flight wouldn't take place for another fifty years, and it'd be another sixty-two years before a plane would successfully cross the Atlantic. In 1857 you had one option for overseas travel: a boat. And when you traveled by boat, it could take anywhere from eight to fourteen weeks to make your way back to Europe from New York City. That's two to three months to think. Two to three months to read. Two to three months to wrestle with the Creator of the universe as you develop a prayer language and read about this God-man, Jesus Christ. When you get back to your homeland you don't just leave Christ in that boat and say, "See you later." Nope. You take him with you. You take him with you as you tell others about Jesus the Christ you discovered on that two- to three-month journey back to your homeland on the other side of the Atlantic.

This great businessman's revival didn't just occur in the United States. It swept all across the world as hearts were transformed for the kingdom of God. There were accounts out of England where entire towns gave their life to Christ. The town was transformed. The people were transformed. The Holy Spirit was ushered in. In fact, in many of these towns, police forces were disbanded. Why? There was no more crime. From where I sit, I believe an Acts principle broke out. The Holy Spirit was allowed to have his way. And when the Holy Spirit is allowed to have his way, step back, because a freight train's a-comin', and you best not miss your shot to jump on board that locomotive. This is exactly what happened to the people of England in 1857. They began to see one another through the lens of Christ as the Holy Spirit was once again free to roam his domain. He was welcomed with open arms by people all across the world as story after story, testimony after testimony began to unfold as they defeated the devil by the "blood of the Lamb [Jesus] and the word of their testimony [story]" (Revelation 12:11).

It's said that as this revival swept across the world, churches were busting at the seams. There was no room in the inn as churches had to move their services outside. Pictures show thousands of people gathered outside as churches moved their services to parks and lakes. People were coming to Christ in droves. In fact, it's said that twenty thousand people were baptized, and more than fifty thousand people were coming to faith in Christ.

Per week!

It's believed that in America over a million people—one million people—died to their old self as they committed to walk with Christ for the rest of their life. The old was gone. The new had come! (2 Corinthians 5:17).

I'd be willing to bet you haven't heard of this great revival. In fact, I've only met a small handful of people who have. You won't find it in textbooks. You most likely won't hear about it in your church. It's been hidden from us. Out of sight, out of mind.

Cloaked.

We've been cloaked by the devil as he has tucked this great awakening that took place in 1857–1858 far from our minds. He doesn't want you to know anything about the businessman's revival of 1857. He desperately doesn't want you to catch wind of this great awakening. It scares him. Check that, it terrifies him.

He's terrified.

Absolutely terrified.
Of God's Holy Spirit imbued in you.

MEDITATIONS WITH ROSWELL

Had you ever heard of the Businessman's Revival of 1857? In what ways do you believe a revival such as this would transform our communities, our country, and our world? Do you believe God can do it again? I believe he can, and I believe he can do it through you, the man or woman filled with God's Holy Spirit!

ABOUT THE AUTHOR

Keith Toogood is a proud native Texan who resides in Lubbock, Texas, with his wife, Brandi, and their three amazing kids. He is a 2006 graduate of the Rawls College of Business at Texas Tech University, where he obtained three degrees: marketing, management, and general business. While attending Texas Tech, Keith was also a kicker on the football team from 2002–2006. During his senior season, he led the Big 12 in touchbacks and finished third nationally during that 2006 campaign. His success on the field that senior season led to workouts with the Bills and Cowboys, but ultimately God had plans for Keith in the world of business.

Currently, Keith is the founder and president of Toogood Built Homes, a custom homebuilding company located in Lubbock, Texas. He is also the founder of BGTX (Build

Group Texas) Construction, a commercial construction company based out of Lubbock. He is a podcast host of The Epicenter with his partner in BOOM (Business Operating on Mission), Roswell Smith Jr. In previous business ventures, he was the founder of Teko Outdoor, an outdoor living construction company that was later sold to his COO and former franchise owner of Orangetheory Fitness.

As the founder of BOOM, Keith has a passion for helping leaders understand their identity and specific calling in God's kingdom as they embark on a mission to impact communities locally and across the globe.

Printed in the USA
CPSIA information can be obtained
at www.ICGtesting.com
CBHW031241190724
11674CB00007B/536